A
CHARLES DICKENS
SELECTION

EDITED BY PETER THOMAS

Heinemann
New Windmills

Heinemann is an imprint of Pearson Education Limited,
a company incorporated in England and Wales, having
its registered office at Edinburgh Gate, Harlow, Essex, CM20 2JE.
Registered company number: 872828

First published in the New Windmill Series 1996

11

ISBN: 978 0 435124 45 8

Text designed by Jim Turner
Typeset by Books Unlimited (Nottm) NG19 7QZ
Cover illustration by John Holder
Cover design by The Point
Printed in China (CTPS/11)

Acknowledgements
The authors and publishers should like to thank the following for
permission to use illustrations.
Fred Barnard/The Dickens House Museum, 30; PHIZ/The Dickens House
Museum, 36; Cruikshank/The Dickens House Museum, 49; Charles
Green/The Dickens House Museum, 63; PHIZ/The Dickens House
Museum, 76; Artist unknown – 'AHW'/The Dickens House Museum, 111;
Cruikshank/The Dickens House Museum, 122; PHIZ/The Dickens House
Museum, 139; Cruikshank/The Dickens House Museum, 182; Artist
unknown/The Dickens House Museum, 190.

Contents

Foreword

If you've never read any Dickens before, this book is for you. If you've imagined that reading Dickens means struggling through hundreds of pages in a foreign language, this book is definitely for you. It's a collection of the best bits of Dickens chosen to make you smile and think.

If you want to know why Dickens is admired as a comic writer, start off with his description of Mr Bumble trying to put his wife in her place.

If you want to know why Dickens is regarded as a writer with a conscience, read his account of life in the condemned cell at Newgate.

And if neither of these is your starting point, check out how well Dickens understood young people and the misery heaped on them by hypocritical adults in *Pip's Christmas dinner*.

Dickens was an entertainer, but he was also a man with a strong sense of moral and social justice. There's crime and corruption in these pages, as well as humour and affection. I hope these extracts show his skill in creating characters, and his sharp eye for social behaviour and, especially, the wrongs of life in Victorian England. It's not just Victorian England that gets the close focus in these pages. You may find ideas and details still true today – which is a reason for calling Dickens a great writer for his age and for ours. Some things don't change – and people today are no less foolish or evil than people were long ago. Writers today describe the good to be found in the shady side of life, and the corruption to be found in the respectable parts, just as writers always have.

Dickens wrote well about the murky underside of Victorian England, but he had a sharp eye for the rituals of the well off and respectable too. He enjoyed describing ridiculous behaviour, but his sense of humour was warm and forgiving, recognizing that all human beings act foolishly at some time or another. He found it easier, though, to show the follies of the wealthy and important, because human beings tend to be most foolish when they take themselves too seriously.

If you like browsing you need not start at the beginning, but can pick a character at random – and see why so many readers have enjoyed the colourful characters that made Dickens famous – Fagin or Mr Pickwick or Mark Tapley or ... well, anyone!

Good reading!

Notes on the selection

Any personal choice of extracts for an anthology will cause enthusiasts or experts to quarrel with it. Some will object to the fact that their favourite scenes, or characters, or novels are left out. Others will object to cuts made in the extracts, or to the way the extracts have been put into groups.

This selection is for newcomers to Dickens, who may or may not become enthusiasts or experts later on in life and reading. It is a personal selection to introduce Dickens' work to a wider audience. I have chosen passages, made cuts, and arranged the groups to suit teachers in classrooms or readers at home. I looked for extracts which are funny to read aloud, good to discuss and also give a range of Dickens' material and style.

Readers can make their own connections if they do not like mine. You may find links between parts taken out of the same novel; or you may find interesting contrasts. I have simply grouped the extracts in a way which shows one thread of similarity. No doubt many of the extracts could be regrouped within this volume. That is one of the pleasures of reading.

I have glossed some words to help the meaning, but where glossing would hinder the reading flow, I have cut words or phrases. I have also cut references to characters who are not necessary to the scene, and parts which do not help the pace in a short extract. If the appetite is whetted, then readers can go to the originals – for the anthology is a sampler and its success will be in bringing new readers to the pleasure of Dickens.

Introduction

Charles Dickens was born in 1812. His father was a clerk working for the Navy Pay office, so his early years gave him plenty of chances to see life along the Thames as he went with his father on boats and around London's docks and inns.

He attended a small school run by a young teacher for a modest fee until he was eleven, when he moved with his family to London. His father was not earning much money and his mother tried to bring some in by starting a small school, but the venture failed. The family had to sell the books they had collected and take more valuable household goods to a pawnshop.

On Charles' twelfth birthday, his parents were pleased to find him a job at Warren's Blacking Factory, a dirty and decayed warehouse overrun with rats. Most of his time was spent in sticking labels on bottles. He hated the job and the place and, even in later life, he looked back on this early experience with bitterness and disgust. Shortly after starting work, Charles found more sadness. His father was arrested for debt and taken to a debtors' prison, soon to be followed by his wife and the five other children.

Charles visited the family regularly in the prison and never forgot the experience of poverty and misery. He was determined to make his own way in life and not repeat the mistakes of his father. Without the advantages of a public school education or university, or friends with money and influence, he had to live on his wits and use his talents. He found himself a job as a solicitor's clerk, then as a reporter. Getting to know the legal and criminal affairs of London confirmed his opinion that life was unjust and that sometimes the law was no better. He saw other people's struggles and he saw that wealth made life easier and poverty made it miserable. He knew the ugly underside of life in the capital at the hub of a great empire.

Dickens became more and more successful as a writer of sketches and stories for newspapers and magazines. Eventually, he wrote novels for his own magazines, becoming wealthy in the process. He wrote many books which pleased readers with their humour and their sentiment and became a best-seller and a popular entertainer, presenting his stories at public readings in this country and in the United States. But he never forgot the misery of his youth, and his novels deal repeatedly with the agonies of growing up, the life of the poor and the workings of British justice.

He died in 1870 and was buried in Westminster Abbey, despite his own request that he should be quietly buried at Gad's Hill with 'no revolting absurdity' of funeral ceremonies.

Dickens the writer

Dickens would have loved television: not watching it, but writing for it. It would have given him a huge audience, and he would have made a fortune writing series that BBC or ITV would have put on at peak viewing times. As it was, he used his talent to make his name and money in the medium that was available before the electric revolution: the monthly magazine.

Most of the novels written during the nineteenth century were published as serials. Charles Dickens became successful as a writer for these magazines – first for *The Morning Chronicle*, and then for *The Monthly Magazine*. He was a winning property as a writer, and editors were keen to get him into their pages. Sales went up when readers got involved in one of Dickens' stories. When he wrote *Oliver Twist*, for example, people who had read about Nancy and Bill Sykes waited anxiously to find out what would happen to them. When the ship bringing copies of the latest instalment of the story arrived in New York, there were crowds on the quay-side not just waiting for family and friends to disembark, but to get hold of the latest episode of the story!

In 1850, Dickens set up a weekly magazine called *Household Words*, which was intended to appeal to a wider readership than the literary journals. In it he published other writers' stories as well as his own. It carried articles on education, the prison system and on social class and privilege, as well as stories. It called itself a 'gentle mouthpiece of reform'. Dickens was now in a position where his creative skill in writing fiction was part of his business income and a way of influencing public opinion in large-scale political matters.

Dickens had always had strong views about what he thought wrong in public life. As he grew in confidence as a writer these views played a bigger part in his work. He had always included episodes and descriptions of injustice and social need in his stories, but with the three great novels of 1852–57, *Bleak House, Hard Times* and *Little Dorrit*, he made social and political wrongs an essential part of the whole.

So, Dickens the public entertainer was becoming more and more a critic of the life around him. He didn't stop making people laugh but he wanted them to think and feel about where the country was going and what was threatening the quality of life and relationships.

1
Adults and children

Throughout his novels, Dickens shows a strong sympathy with children as victims of adult behaviour. Although Victorian England liked to think that it had strong family values, Dickens shows a different side – of misunderstanding, neglect and hypocrisy. He knew that children suffer more than adults can guess, even in respectable homes, if parents have little time or affection for their children. He also knew that children see adults' faults more clearly than adults do. At the start of *David Copperfield*, he wrote:

> I believe the power of observation in numbers of very young children to be quite wonderful for its closeness and accuracy.

Dickens also felt that children have a strong sense of morality, and are easily hurt by unjust treatment. In *Great Expectations*, he wrote:

> In the little world in which children have their existence, whosoever brings them up, there is nothing so finely perceived, and so finely felt, as injustice. It may be only small injustice that the child is exposed to; but the child is small and its world is small, and its rocking-horse stands as many hands high, according to scale, as a big-boned Irish hunter.

In these extracts, by putting the reader into the child's position, Dickens shows how children can suffer from adult insensitivity. But it's not all misery: he does it with humour as well as passion. As always with Dickens, he shows that there are some redeeming kindnesses in a cruel world.

Practical parenting and the Pocket family

The Pocket household is a reminder that disease and poverty are not the only kinds of deprivation to affect children. Here there is neglect in the middle of comfort, where the children are not so much brought up but allowed to 'tumble up'.
Mr Pocket is a lecturer in domestic economy, which makes his failure to organize and manage anything more amusing. Mrs Pocket dreams of becoming a Lady, spending more time reading about Titles than talking to her children. They have no idea of how to care for their large family – and it is left to servants and the children themselves to provide affection and responsibility.

After dinner the children were introduced. There were four little girls, and two little boys, besides the baby who might have been either, and the baby's next successor who was as yet neither. They were brought in by Flopson and Millers, much as though those two non-commissioned officers had been recruiting somewhere for children and had enlisted these: while Mrs Pocket looked as if she thought she had had the pleasure of inspecting them before, but didn't quite know what to make of them.

'Here! Give me your fork, Mum, and take the baby,' said Flopson. 'Don't take it that way, or you'll get its head under the table.'

Thus advised, Mrs Pocket took it the other way, and got its head upon the table; which was announced to all present by a **prodigious concussion**.

'Dear, dear! Give it me back, Mum,' said Flopson; 'and Miss Jane, come and dance to baby, do!'

One of the little girls, a mere mite who seemed to have prematurely taken upon herself some charge of the others, stepped out of her place by me, and danced to and from the baby until it left off crying, and laughed. Then, all the children laughed, and Mr Pocket (who in the meantime had twice endeavoured to lift himself up by the hair) laughed, and we all laughed and were glad.

Flopson, by doubling the baby at the joints like a Dutch doll, then got it safely into Mrs Pocket's lap, and gave it the nut-crackers to play with: at the same time recommending Mrs Pocket to take notice that the handles of that instrument were not likely to agree with its eyes, and sharply charging Miss Jane to look after the same. Then, the two nurses left the room, and had a lively scuffle on the staircase with a **dissipated** page who had waited at dinner, and who had clearly lost half his buttons at the gaming-table.

I was made very uneasy in my mind by Mrs Pocket's falling into a discussion respecting two **baronetcies**, while she ate a sliced orange steeped in sugar and wine, and forgetting all about the baby on her lap: who did most appalling things with the nut-crackers. At length, little Jane perceiving its young brains to be **imperilled**, softly left her place, and with many small

---

Glossary

prodigious concussion: loud bang

dissipated: low-living, depraved

baronetcies: the lowest level of hereditary peerage

imperilled: in danger

artifices coaxed the dangerous weapon away. Mrs Pocket finished her orange at about the same time, and not approving of this, said to Jane –

'You naughty child, how dare you? Go and sit down this instant!'

'Mamma dear,' lisped the little girl, 'baby ood have put hith eyeth out.'

'How dare you tell me so?' retorted Mrs Pocket. 'Go and sit down in your chair this moment!'

'Belinda,' remonstrated Mr Pocket, from the other end of the table, 'how can you be so unreasonable? Jane only interfered for the protection of baby.'

'I will not allow anybody to interfere,' said Mrs Pocket. 'I am surprised, Matthew, that you should expose me to the **affront** of interference.'

'Good God!' cried Mr Pocket, in an outburst of desolate desperation. 'Are infants to be nut-crackered into their tombs, and is nobody to save them?'

'I will not be interfered with by Jane,' said Mrs Pocket, with a majestic glance at that innocent little offender.

Mr Pocket got his hands in his hair again, and this time really did lift himself some inches out of his chair. 'Hear this!' he helplessly explained to the elements. Then he let himself down again, and became silent.

We all looked awkwardly at the tablecloth while this was going on. A pause succeeded, during which the honest and irrepressible baby made a series of leaps and crows at little Jane, who appeared to me to be the only member of the family (**irrespective** of servants) **with whom it had any decided acquaintance**.

Mrs Pocket said, 'Will you ring for Flopson? Jane, you undutiful little thing, go and lie down. Now, baby darling, come with ma!'

The baby protested with all its might. It doubled

itself up the wrong way over Mrs Pocket's arm, exhibited a pair of knitted shoes and dimpled ankles to the company **in lieu** of its soft face, and was carried out in the highest state of mutiny. And it gained its point after all, for I saw it through the window, within a few minutes, being nursed by little Jane.

It happened that the other five children were left behind at the dinner-table, through Flopson's having some private engagement, and their not being anybody else's business. I thus became aware of the mutual relations between them and Mr Pocket, which were exemplified in the following manner. Mr Pocket, with the normal perplexity of his face heightened and his hair rumpled, looked at them for some minutes, as if he couldn't make out how they came to be boarding and lodging in that establishment, and why they hadn't been billeted by Nature on somebody else. Then, in a distant, Missionary way he asked them certain questions – as why little Joe had that hole in his frill: who said, Pa, Flopson was going to mend it when she had time – and how little Fanny came by that **whitlow**: who said, Pa, Millers was going to **poultice** it

---

Glossary

artifices: clever devices

affront: insult or offence

irrespective: leaving aside, apart from

with whom it had any decided acquaintance: whom it knew at all

in lieu: in place of, instead of

whitlow: an abscess of a finger tip caused by infection

poultice: to cover with a thick, hot paste (often bread) with a bandage on top, as a cure for infection

when she didn't forget. Then, he melted into parental tenderness, and gave them a shilling apiece and told them to go and play; and then as they went out, with one very strong effort to lift himself up by the hair, he dismissed the hopeless subject.

Great Expectations

David sees his mother's happiness slip away

Some years after her husband's death, David Copperfield's mother marries Mr Murdstone, who then brings his sister to stay with them. David first of all feels he has lost his mother to Mr Murdstone, then he sees her lose her place in the house and in her new husband's affections. The unhappy child becomes aware of the unhappiness that adults, too, can suffer.

It was Miss Murdstone who was arrived, and a gloomy-looking lady she was; dark, like her brother, whom she greatly resembled in face and voice; and with very heavy eyebrows, nearly meeting over her large nose. She brought with her, two uncompromising hard black boxes, with her initials on the lids in hard brass nails. When she paid the coachman she took her money out of a hard steel purse, and she kept the purse in a very jail of a bag which hung upon her arm by a heavy chain, and shut up like a bite. I had never, at that time, seen such a metallic lady altogether as Miss Murdstone was.

She was brought into the parlour with many tokens of welcome, and there formally recognized my mother as a new and near relation. Then she looked at me, and said:

'Is that your boy, sister-in-law?'

My mother acknowledged me.

'Generally speaking,' said Miss Murdstone, 'I don't like boys. How d'ye do, boy?'

Under these encouraging circumstances, I replied that I was very well, and that I hoped she was the same; with such an **indifferent grace**, that Miss Murdstone disposed of me in two words:

'Wants manner!'

Having uttered which, she begged the favour of being shown to her room, which became to me from that time forth a place of awe and dread, wherein the two black boxes were never seen open or known to be left unlocked, and where (for I peeped in once or twice when she was out) numerous little steel **fetters and rivets**, with which Miss Murdstone embellished herself when she was dressed, generally hung upon the looking-glass in **formidable array**.

As well as I could make out, she had come for good, and had no intention of ever going again. She began to 'help' my mother next morning, and was in and out of the store-closet all day, putting things to rights, and making havoc in the old arrangements. Almost the first remarkable thing I observed in Miss Murdstone was her being constantly haunted by a suspicion that the servants had a man secreted somewhere on the premises. Under the influence of this delusion, she dived into the coal-cellar at the most untimely hours, and scarcely ever opened the door of a dark cupboard without clapping it to again, in the belief that she had got him.

Though there was nothing very airy about Miss Murdstone, she was a perfect Lark in point of getting up. She was up before anybody in the house was stirring. Peggotty gave it as her opinion that she even slept with one eye open; but I could not **concur** in this idea; for I tried it myself after hearing the suggestion thrown out, and found it couldn't be done.

On the very first morning after her arrival she was up and ringing her bell at cock-crow. When my mother came down to breakfast and was going to make the tea, Miss Murdstone gave her a kind of peck on the cheek, which was her nearest approach to a kiss, and said:

'Now, Clara, my dear, I am come here, you know, to relieve you of all the trouble I can. You're much too pretty and thoughtless' – my mother blushed but laughed, and seemed not to dislike this character – 'to have any duties imposed upon you that can be undertaken by me. If you'll be so good as give me your keys, my dear, I'll attend to all this sort of thing in future.'

From that time, Miss Murdstone kept the keys in her own little jail all day, and under her pillow all night, and my mother had no more to do with them than I had.

My mother did not **suffer** her authority to pass from her without a shadow of protest. One night when Miss Murdstone had been developing certain household plans to her brother, of which he signified his **approbation**, my mother suddenly began to cry, and said she thought she might have been consulted.

Glossary

indifferent grace: in an off-hand way

fetters and rivets: chains and bolts – it is really Miss Murdstone's jewellery

formidable array: impressive arrangement

concur: fall in with, agree

suffer: allow

approbation: approval

'Clara!' said Mr Murdstone sternly. 'Clara! I wonder at you.'

'Oh, it's very well to say you wonder, Edward!' cried my mother, 'and it's very well for you to talk about firmness, but you wouldn't like it yourself.'

Firmness, I may observe, was the grand quality on which both Mr and Miss Murdstone took their stand.

'It's very hard,' said my mother, 'that in my own house –'

'*My* own house?' repeated Mr Murdstone. 'Clara!'

'*Our* own house, I mean,' faltered my mother, evidently frightened – 'I hope you must know what I mean, Edward – it's very hard that in *your* own house I may not have a word to say about domestic matters. I am sure I managed very well before we were married. There's evidence,' said my mother, sobbing; 'ask Peggotty if I didn't do very well when I wasn't interfered with!'

'Edward,' said Miss Murdstone, 'let there be an end of this. I go tomorrow.'

'Jane Murdstone,' said her brother, 'be silent! How dare you to insinuate that you don't know my character better than your words imply?'

'I am sure,' my poor mother went on, at a grievous disadvantage, and with many tears, 'I don't want anybody to go. I should be very miserable and unhappy if anybody was to go. I don't ask much. I am not unreasonable. I only want to be consulted sometimes. I am very much obliged to anybody who assists me, and I only want to be consulted as a mere form, sometimes. I thought you were pleased, once, with my being a little inexperienced and girlish, Edward – I am sure you said so – but you seem to hate me for it now, you are so severe.'

'Edward,' said Miss Murdstone, again, 'let there be an end of this. I go tomorrow.'

'Jane Murdstone,' thundered Mr Murdstone. 'Will you be silent? How dare you?'

Miss Murdstone made a jail-delivery of her pocket-handkerchief, and held it before her eyes.

'Clara,' he continued, looking at my mother, 'you surprise me! You astound me! Yes, I had a satisfaction in the thought of marrying an inexperienced and **artless** person, and forming her character, and **infusing** into it some amount of that firmness of which it stood in need. But when Jane Murdstone is kind enough to come to my assistance in this **endeavour**, and to assume, for my sake, a condition something like a housekeeper's, and when she meets with a base return –'

'Oh, pray, pray, Edward,' cried my mother, 'don't accuse me of being ungrateful. I am sure I am not ungrateful. No one ever said I was before. I have many faults, but not that. Oh, don't, my dear!'

'When Jane Murdstone meets, I say,' he went on, after waiting until my mother was silent, 'with a base return, that feeling of mine is chilled and altered.'

'Don't, my love, say that!' implored my mother very piteously. 'Oh, don't, Edward! I can't bear to hear it. Whatever I am, I am affectionate. I know I am affectionate. I wouldn't say it, if I wasn't sure that I am. Ask Peggotty. I am sure she'll tell you I'm affectionate.'

┌ Glossary

artless: natural, unselfconscious, the opposite of scheming
infusing: putting in
endeavour: task, enterprise

'There is no extent of mere weakness, Clara,' said Mr Murdstone in reply, 'that can have the least weight with me. You lose breath.'

'Pray let us be friends,' said my mother, 'I couldn't live under coldness or unkindness. I am so sorry. I have a great many defects, I know, and it's very good of you, Edward, with your strength of mind, to **endeavour** to correct them for me. Jane, I don't object to anything. I should be quite broken-hearted if you thought of leaving –' My mother was too much overcome to go on.

'Jane Murdstone,' said Mr Murdstone to his sister, 'any harsh words between us are, I hope, uncommon. It is not my fault that so unusual an occurrence has taken place tonight. I was betrayed into it by another. Nor is it your fault. You were betrayed into it by another. Let us both try to forget it. And as this,' he added, after these **magnanimous** words, 'is not a fit scene for the boy – David, go to bed!'

I could hardly find the door, through the tears that stood in my eyes. I was so sorry for my mother's distress; but I groped my way out, and groped my way up to my room in the dark, without even having the heart to say good night to Peggotty, or to get a candle from her. When her coming up to look for me, an hour or so afterwards, awoke me, she said that my mother had gone to bed poorly, and that Mr and Miss Murdstone were sitting alone.

Going down next morning rather earlier than usual, I paused outside the parlour door, on hearing my mother's voice. She was very earnestly and humbly **entreating** Miss Murdstone's pardon, which that lady granted, and a perfect **reconciliation** took place. I never knew my mother afterwards to give an opinion on any matter, without first appealing to Miss Murdstone, or without having first ascertained by some sure means, what Miss Murdstone's opinion was; and I never saw Miss Murdstone, when out of temper (she was infirm that way), move her hand towards her bag as if she were going to take out the keys and offer to resign them to my mother, without seeing that my mother was in a terrible fright.

David Copperfield

Glossary

endeavour: to try
magnanimous: generous in a lordly way
entreating: begging, pleading
reconciliation: come to agreement again

Season of Goodwill and victimizing the young: Pip's Christmas dinner

This Christmas dinner is an unhappy affair for young Pip. An orphan, he has been brought up by his shrewish sister, Mrs Joe, and her gentle husband, Joe. On this occasion, Mrs Joe's friends, Wopsle, Pumblechook and the Hubbles, tuck in with relish to two pleasures: stuffing themselves and preaching at youngsters in general (and Pip in particular) for faults such as greed and ingratitude. Throughout, Joe tries to make up for the insensitivity and hypocrisy of the others in the only way he can without being noticed.

I opened the door to the company – making believe that it was a habit of ours to open that door – and I opened it first to Mr Wopsle, next to Mr and Mrs Hubble, and last of all to Uncle Pumblechook. N.B. – *I* was not allowed to call him uncle, under the severest penalties.

'Mrs Joe,' said Uncle Pumblechook: a large hard-breathing, middle-aged, slow man, with a mouth like a fish, dull staring eyes, and sandy hair standing upright on his head, so that he looked as if he had just been all but choked, and had that moment come to; 'I have brought you, as the compliments of the season – I have brought you, Mum, a bottle of sherry wine – and I have brought you, Mum, a bottle of port wine.'

Every Christmas Day he presented himself, as a **profound novelty**, with exactly the same words, and carrying the two bottles like dumb-bells. Every Christ-

mas Day, Mrs Joe replied, as she now replied, 'Oh. Un –
cle Pum – ble – chook! This is kind!' Every Christmas
Day, he retorted, as he now retorted, 'It's no more
than your merits. And now are you all **bobbish**, and
how's Sixpennorth of halfpence?' meaning me.

We dined on these occasions in the kitchen, and
adjourned, for the nuts and oranges and apples, to the
parlour; which was a change very like Joe's change
from his working clothes to his Sunday dress. My sister was uncommonly lively on the present occasion,
and indeed was generally more gracious in the society
of Mrs Hubble than in any other company. I remember
Mrs Hubble as a little, curly, sharp-edged person in
sky-blue, who held a conventionally juvenile position,
because she had married Mr Hubble – I don't know at
what remote period – when she was much younger
than he. I remember Mr Hubble as a tough, high-
shouldered, stooping old man, of a saw-dusty fra-
grance, with his legs extraordinarily wide apart: so
that in my short days I always saw some miles of open
country between them when I met him coming up the
lane.

Among this good company I should have felt myself,
even if I hadn't robbed the pantry, in a false position.
Not because I was squeezed in at an acute angle of
the tablecloth, with the table in my chest, and the
Pumblechookian elbow in my eye, nor because I was

Glossary

profound novelty: something startlingly new

bobbish: cheerful and well

adjourned: stopped, in order to move to another place and
  continue

not allowed to speak (I didn't want to speak), nor because I was **regaled with** the scaly tips of the drumsticks of the fowl, and with those obscure corners of pork of which the pig, when living, had the least reason to be vain. No; I should not have minded that, if they would only have left me alone. But they wouldn't leave me alone. They seemed to think the opportunity lost, if they failed to point the conversation at me, every now and then, and stick the point into me. I might have been an unfortunate little bull in a Spanish arena, I got so smartingly touched up by these moral **goads**.

It began the moment we sat down to dinner. Mr Wopsle said grace with theatrical declamation – as it now appears to me, something like a religious cross of the Ghost in 'Hamlet' with 'Richard the Third' – and ended with the very proper **aspiration** that we might be truly grateful. Upon which my sister fixed me with her eye, and said, in a low, reproachful voice, 'Do you hear that? Be grateful.'

'Especially,' said Mr Pumblechook, 'be grateful, boy, to them which brought you up by hand.'

Mrs Hubble shook her head, and **contemplating** me with a mournful **presentiment** that I should come to no good, asked, 'Why is it that the young are never grateful?' This moral mystery seemed too much for the company until Mr Hubble **tersely** solved it by saying, 'Naturally vicious.' Everybody then murmured, 'True!' and looked at me in a particularly unpleasant and personal manner.

Joe's station and influence were something feebler (if possible), when there was company, than when there was none. But he always aided and comforted me when he could, in some way of his own, and he always did so at dinner-time by giving me gravy, if there were any. There being plenty of gravy today, Joe spooned into my plate, at this point, about half a pint.

A little later on in the dinner, Mr Wopsle reviewed the sermon with some severity, and intimated – in the usual hypothetical case of the Church being '**thrown open**' – what kind of sermon *he* would have given them. After favouring them with some heads of that discourse, he remarked that he considered the subject of the day's **homily** ill-chosen; which was the less excusable, he added, when there were so many subjects 'going about'.

'True again,' said Uncle Pumblechook. 'You've hit it, sir! Plenty of subjects going about, for them that know how to put salt upon their tails. That's what's wanted. A man needn't go far to find a subject, if he's ready with his salt-box.' Mr Pumblechook added, after a short interval of reflection, 'Look at Pork alone. There's a subject! If you want a subject, look at Pork!'

'True, sir. Many a moral for the young,' returned Mr Wopsle; and I knew he was going to lug me in, before he said it; 'might be deduced from that text.'

Glossary

regaled with: treated to

goads: sticks with sharp points, used on animals to make them move faster

aspiration: hopeful wish

contemplating: looking at in a thoughtful way

presentiment: premonition, glimpse of the future

tersely: briefly and roughly

'thrown open': Mr Wopsle would like the job of vicar to be open for anyone to apply for

homily: sermon

('You listen to this,') said my sister to me, in a severe parenthesis.

Joe gave me some more gravy.

'Swine,' pursued Mr Wopsle, in his deepest voice, and pointing his fork at my blushes, as if he were mentioning my Christian name; 'Swine were the companions of the prodigal. The gluttony of Swine is put before us, as an example to the young.' (I thought this pretty well in him who had been praising up the pork for being so plump and juicy.) 'What is detestable in a pig, is more detestable in a boy.'

'Or girl,' suggested Mr Hubble.

'Of course, or girl, Mr Hubble,' assented Mr Wopsle, rather irritably, 'but there is no girl present.'

'Besides,' said Mr Pumblechook, turning sharp on me, 'think what you've got to be grateful for. If you'd been born a Squeaker –'

'He *was*, if ever a child was,' said my sister most emphatically.

Joe gave me some more gravy.

'Well, but I mean a four-footed Squeaker,' said Mr Pumblechook. 'If you had been born such, would you have been here now. Not you –'

'Unless in that form,' said Mr Wopsle, nodding towards the dish.

'But I don't mean in that form, sir,' returned Mr Pumblechook, who had an objection to being interrupted; 'I mean, enjoying myself with his elders and betters, and improving himself with their conversation, and rolling in the lap of luxury. Would he have been doing that? No, he wouldn't. And what would have been your destination?' turning on me again. 'You would have been disposed of for so many shillings, according to the market price of the article, and Dunstable the butcher would have come up to you as you lay in your straw, and he would have whipped you under his left arm, and with his right he would have tucked up his frock to get a pen-knife from out of his waistcoat-pocket, and he would have shed your blood and had your life. No bringing up by hand then. Not a bit of it!'

Joe offered me more gravy, which I was afraid to take.

'He was a world of trouble to you, ma'am,' said Mrs Hubble, **commiserating** my sister.

'Trouble?' echoed my sister; 'trouble?' And then entered on a fearful catalogue of all the illnesses I had been guilty of, and all the acts of sleeplessness I had committed, and all the high places I had tumbled from, and all the low places I had tumbled into, and all the injuries I had done myself, and all the times she had wished me in my grave, and I had refused to go there.

I think the Romans must have aggravated one another very much with their noses. Perhaps, they became the restless people they were, in consequence. Anyhow, Mr Wopsle's Roman nose so aggravated me during the recital of my **misdemeanours**, that I should have liked to pull it until he howled. But, all I had endured up to this time, was nothing in comparison with the awful feelings that took possession of me when the pause was broken which ensued upon my sister's recital, and in which pause everybody had looked at me (as I felt painfully conscious) with indignation and **abhorrence**.

Glossary

commiserating: sympathizing with
misdemeanour: minor crime or misbehaviour
abhorrence: loathing

'Yet,' said Mr Pumblechook, leading the company gently back to the theme from which they had strayed, 'Pork – regarded as **biled** – is rich, too; ain't it?'

'Have a little brandy, uncle,' said my sister.

O Heavens, it had come at last! He would find it was weak, he would say it was weak, and I was lost! I held tight to the leg of the table under the cloth, with both hands, and awaited my fate.

My sister went for the stone bottle, came back with the stone bottle, and poured his brandy out: no one else taking any. The wretched man trifled with his glass – took it up, looked at it through the light, put it down – prolonged my misery. All this time, Mrs Joe and Joe were briskly clearing the table for the pie and pudding.

I couldn't keep my eyes off him. Always holding tight by the leg of the table with my hands and feet, I saw the miserable creature finger his glass playfully, take it up, smile, throw his head back, and drink the brandy off. Instantly afterwards, the company were seized with unspeakable **consternation**, owing to his springing to his feet, turning round several times in an appalling **spasmodic** whooping-cough dance, and rushing out at the door; he then became visible through the window, violently plunging and **expectorating**, making the most hideous faces, and apparently out of his mind.

I held on tight, while Mrs Joe and Joe ran to him. I didn't know how I had done it, but I had no doubt I had murdered him somehow. In my dreadful situation, it was a relief when he was brought back, and, surveying the company all round as if *they* had disagreed with him, sank down into his chair with the one significant gasp, 'Tar!'

I had filled up the bottle from the Tar-water jug. I

knew he would be worse by and by. I moved the table, like a Medium of the present day, by the vigour of my unseen hold upon it.

'Tar!' cried my sister in amazement. 'Why, however could Tar come here?'

But, Uncle Pumblechook, who was **omnipotent** in that kitchen, wouldn't hear the word, wouldn't hear the subject, **imperiously** waved it all away with his hand, and asked for hot gin-and-water. My sister, who had begun to be alarmingly meditative, had to employ herself actively in getting the gin, the hot water, the sugar, and the lemon-peel, and mixing them. For the time at least, I was saved. I still held on to the leg of the table, but clutched it now with the **fervour** of gratitude.

By degrees, I became calm enough to release my grasp and **partake** of pudding. Mr Pumblechook partook of pudding. All partook of pudding. The course terminated, and Mr Pumblechook had begun to beam under the **genial** influence of gin-and-water. I began to think I should get over the day, when my sister said to Joe, 'Clean plates – cold.'

Glossary

biled: boiled
consternation: concern, anxiety
spasmodic: jerky
expectorating: spitting
omnipotent: all-powerful
imperiously: in a grandly commanding way
fervour: passionately strong feeling
partake: have a share of, eat
genial: cheering

I clutched the leg of the table again immediately, and pressed it to my bosom as if it had been the companion of my youth and friend of my soul. I foresaw what was coming, and I felt that this time I really was gone.

'You must taste,' said my sister, addressing the guests with her best grace, 'you must taste, to finish with, such a delightful and delicious present of Uncle Pumblechook's!'

Must they! Let them not hope to taste it!

'You must know,' said my sister, rising, 'it's a pie; a savoury pork pie.'

The company murmured their compliments. Uncle Pumblechook, sensible of having deserved well of his fellow-creatures, said – quite vivaciously, all things considered, 'Well, Mrs Joe, we'll do our best endeavours; let us have a cut at this same pie.'

My sister went out to get it. I heard her steps proceed to the pantry. I saw Mr Pumblechook balance his knife. I saw reawakening appetite in the Roman nostrils of Mr Wopsle. I heard Mr Hubble remark that 'a bit of savoury pork pie would lay atop of anything you could mention, and do no harm,' and I heard Joe say, 'You shall have some, Pip.' I have never been absolutely certain whether I uttered a shrill yell of terror, merely in spirit, or in the bodily hearing of the company. I felt that I could bear no more, and that I must run away. I released the leg of the table and ran for my life.

But, I ran no farther than the house door, for there I ran head foremost into a party of soldiers with their muskets; one of whom held out a pair of handcuffs to me, saying, 'Here you are, look sharp, come on!'

Great Expectations

2
Lessons and learning

Some of the best-known passages from Dickens' novels are those dealing with life in the schoolroom. Teachers do not emerge well from these descriptions – and education seems nothing to do with the pleasure of learning or developing one's talents. Dickens presents a bleak view of schools as institutions for oppressing and repressing young people. People in Victorian England believed they were doing what was best for the children. But they were gripped by an idea which was widespread at that time – that children were empty vessels, containing nothing worthwhile until filled with what adults judged best.

Individuals do damage too, of course. The individuals who feature in Dotheboys Hall are greedy exploiters – people who see education as a trade, a way of making money by offering a service or convenience to parents, relieving them of the tiresome need to bring up their children, and making a fine profit at little cost in the meantime.

When reading these extracts, you may begin to ask yourself how much attitudes have changed since Dickens wrote, and how far you can find today any traces of thinking about children and school which Dickens would recognize if he came back to life.

Mr Murdstone teaches David a lesson

David Copperfield's father died and his mother later married Mr Murdstone, a harsh and unsympathetic man who believes he knows what's best in developing a child's character and intelligence.

Shall I ever forget those lessons! They were presided over nominally by my mother, but really by Mr Murdstone and his sister, who were always present, and found them a favourable occasion for giving my mother lessons in that miscalled firmness, which was the bane of both our lives. I believe I was kept at home for that purpose. I had been apt enough to learn, and willing enough, when my mother and I had lived alone together. I can faintly remember learning the alphabet at her knee. But these solemn lessons I remember as the death-blow of my peace, and a grievous daily drudgery and misery. They were very long, very numerous, very hard – perfectly unintelligible, some of them, to me – and I was generally as much bewildered by them as I believe my poor mother was herself.

Let me remember how it used to be, and bring one morning back again.

I come into the second-best parlour after breakfast, with my books, and an exercise-book, and a slate. My mother is ready for me at her writing-desk, but not half so ready as Mr Murdstone in his easy-chair by the window (though he pretends to be reading a book), or as Miss Murdstone, sitting near my mother stringing steel beads. The very sight of these two has such an influence over me, that I begin to feel the words I have been at infinite pains to get into my head all sliding away, and going I don't know where. I wonder where they *do* go, by the by?

I hand the first book to my mother. Perhaps it is a grammar, perhaps a history, or geography. I take a last drowning look at the page as I give it into her hand, and start off aloud at a racing pace while I have got it fresh. I trip over a word. Mr Murdstone looks up. I trip over another word. Miss Murdstone looks up. I redden, tumble over half-a-dozen words, and stop. I think my mother would show me the book if she dared, but she does not dare, and she says softly:

'Oh, Davy, Davy!'

'Now, Clara,' says Mr Murdstone, 'be firm with the boy. Don't say, "Oh, Davy, Davy!" That's childish. He knows his lesson, or he does not know it.'

'He does *not* know it,' Miss Murdstone interposes awfully.

'I am really afraid he does not,' says my mother.

'Then, you see, Clara,' returns Miss Murdstone, 'you should just give him the book back, and make him know it.'

'Yes, certainly,' says my mother; 'that is what I intend to do, my dear Jane. Now, Davy, try once more, and don't be stupid.'

I obey the first clause of the **injunction** by trying once more, but am not so successful with the second, for I am very stupid. I tumble down before I get to the

---

Glossary

injunction: order

old place, at a point where I was all right before, and stop to think. But I can't think about the lesson. I think of the number of yards of net in Miss Murdstone's cap, or of the price of Mr Murdstone's dressing-gown, or any such ridiculous problem that I have no business with, and don't want to have anything at all to do with. Mr Murdstone makes a movement of impatience which I have been expecting for a long time. Miss Murdstone does the same. My mother glances submissively at them, shuts the book, and lays it by as an **arrears** to be worked out when my other tasks are done.

There is a pile of these arrears very soon, and it swells like a rolling snowball. The bigger it gets, the more stupid *I* get. The case is so hopeless, and I feel that I am wallowing in such a bog of nonsense, that I give up all idea of getting out and abandon myself to my fate. The despairing way in which my mother and I look at each other, as I blunder on, is truly melancholy. But the greatest effect in these miserable lessons is when my mother (thinking nobody is observing her) tries to give me the cue by the motion of her lips. At that instant, Miss Murdstone, who has been lying in wait for nothing else all along, says in a deep warning voice:

'Clara!'

My mother starts, colours, and smiles faintly. Mr Murdstone comes out of his chair, takes the book, throws it at me or boxes my ears with it, and turns me out of the room by the shoulders.

Even when the lessons are done, the worst is yet to happen, in the shape of an appalling sum. This is invented for me, and delivered to me **orally** by Mr Murdstone, and begins, 'If I go into a cheesemonger's shop, and buy five thousand double-Gloucester cheeses at fourpence-halfpenny each, present payment' – at which I see Miss Murdstone secretly overjoyed. I pore over these cheeses without any result or enlightenment until dinner-time, when, having made a **Mulatto** of myself by getting the dirt of the slate into the pores of my skin, I have a slice of bread to help me out with the cheeses, and am considered in disgrace for the rest of the evening.

It seems to me, at this distance of time, as if my unfortunate studies generally took this course. I could have done very well if I had been without the Murdstones; but the influence of the Murdstones upon me was like the fascination of two snakes on a wretched young bird. Even when I did get through the morning with tolerable credit, there was not much gained but dinner; for Miss Murdstone never could endure to see me untasked, and if I rashly made any show of being unemployed, called her brother's attention to me by saying, 'Clara, my dear, there's nothing like work – give your boy an exercise'; which caused me some new labour, there and then. As to any recreation with other children of my age, I had very little of that; for the gloomy theology of the Murdstones made all children out to be a swarm of little vipers and held that they contaminated one another.

The natural result of this treatment, continued, I suppose, for some six months or more, was to make me sullen, dull, and dogged. I was not made the less so by

---

Glossary

arrears: backlog

orally: by word of mouth

Mulatto: dark skinned person, usually of mixed European/ African parents

my sense of being daily more and more shut out and alienated from my mother. I believe I should have been almost stupefied but for one circumstance.

It was this. My father had left a small collection of books in a little room upstairs, to which I had access and which nobody else in our house ever troubled. From that blessed little room, Roderick Random, Peregrine Pickle, Humphrey Clinker, Tom Jones, the Vicar of Wakefield, Don Quixote, and Robinson Crusoe came out, a glorious host, to keep me company. They kept alive my fancy, and my hope of something beyond that place and time – they, and the *Arabian Nights*, and did me no harm. It is astonishing to me now, how I found time, in the midst of my porings and blunderings over heavier themes, to read those books as I did. It is curious to me how I could ever have consoled myself under my small troubles (which were great troubles to me), by impersonating my favourite characters in them – as I did – and by putting Mr and Miss Murdstone into all the bad ones – which I did too.

This was my only and my constant comfort. When I think of it, the picture always rises in my mind of a summer evening, the boys at play in the churchyard, and I sitting on my bed, reading as if for life.

One morning when I went into the parlour with my books, I found my mother looking anxious, Miss Murdstone looking firm, and Mr Murdstone binding something round the bottom of a cane – a lithe and limber cane, which he left off binding when I came in, and poised and switched in the air.

'I tell you, Clara,' said Mr Murdstone, 'I have been often flogged myself.'

'To be sure; of course,' said Miss Murdstone.

'Certainly, my dear Jane,' faltered my mother, meekly. 'But – but do you think it did Edward good?'

'Do you think it did Edward harm, Clara?' asked Mr Murdstone, gravely.

'That's the point,' said his sister.

To this my mother returned, 'Certainly, my dear Jane,' and said no more.

I felt apprehensive in this dialogue, and sought Mr Murdstone's eye as it lighted on mine.

'Now, David,' he said 'you must be far more careful today than usual.' He gave the cane another poise, and another switch; and having finished his preparation of it, laid it down beside him, with an impressive look, and took up his book.

This was a good freshener to my presence of mind, as a beginning. I felt the words of my lessons slipping off, not one by one, or line by line, but by the entire page; I tried to lay hold of them; but they seemed, if I may so express it, to have put skates on, and to skim away from me with a smoothness there was no checking.

We began badly, and went on worse. I had come in with an idea of distinguishing myself rather, conceiving that I was very well prepared; but it turned out to be quite a mistake. Book after book was added to the heap of failures, Miss Murdstone being firmly watchful of us all the time. And when we came at last to the five thousand cheeses (canes he made it that day, I remember), my mother burst out crying.

'Clara!' said Miss Murdstone, in her warning voice.

'I am not quite well, my dear Jane, I think,' said my mother.

I saw him wink, solemnly, at his sister, as he rose and said, taking up the cane:

'Why, Jane, we can hardly expect Clara to bear, with perfect firmness, the worry and torment that David has occasioned her today. Clara is greatly strengthened and improved, but we can hardly expect so much from her. David, you and I will go upstairs, boy.'

And when we came at last to the five thousand cheeses (canes he made it that day, I remember), my mother burst out crying

As he took me out at the door, my mother ran towards us. Miss Murdstone said, 'Clara! are you a perfect fool?' and interfered. I saw my mother stop her ears then, and I heard her crying.

He walked me up to my room slowly and gravely – I am certain he had a delight in that formal parade of executing justice – and when we got there, suddenly twisted my head under his arm.

'Mr Murdstone! Sir!' I cried to him. 'Don't! Pray don't beat me! I have tried to learn, sir, but I can't learn while you and Miss Murdstone are by. I can't indeed!'

'Can't you, indeed, David?' he said. 'We'll try that.'

He had my head as in a vice, but I twined round him somehow, and stopped him for a moment, entreating him not to beat me. It was only a moment that I stopped him, for he cut me heavily an instant afterwards, and in the same instant I caught the hand with which he held me in my mouth, between my teeth, and bit it through. It sets my teeth on edge to think of it.

He beat me then, as if he would have beaten me to death. Above all the noise we made, I heard them running up the stairs, and crying out – I heard my mother crying out – and Peggotty. Then he was gone; and the door was locked outside; and I was lying, fevered and hot, and torn, and sore, and raging in my puny way, upon the floor.

How well I recollect, when I became quiet, what an unnatural stillness seemed to reign through the whole house! How well I remember, when my smart and passion began to cool, how wicked I began to feel!

I sat listening for a long while, but there was not a sound. I crawled up from the floor, and saw my face in the glass, so swollen, red, and ugly that it almost frightened me. My stripes were sore and stiff, and

made me cry afresh, when I moved; but they were
nothing to the guilt I felt. It lay heavier on my breast
than if I had been a most atrocious criminal, I dare say.

It had begun to grow dark, and I had shut the window (I had been lying, for the most part, with my head
upon the sill, by turns crying, dozing, and looking listlessly out), when the key was turned, and Miss Murdstone came in with some bread and meat, and milk.
These she put down upon the table without a word,
glaring at me the while with exemplary firmness, and
then retired, locking the door after her.

Long after it was dark I sat there, wondering
whether anybody else would come. When this appeared improbable for that night, I undressed, and
went to bed; and, there, I began to wonder fearfully
what would be done to me. Whether it was a criminal
act that I had committed? Whether I should be taken
into custody, and sent to prison? Whether I was at all
in danger of being hanged?

I never shall forget the waking, next morning; the
being cheerful and fresh for the first moment, and
then the being weighed down by the stale and dismal
oppression of remembrance. Miss Murdstone reappeared before I was out of bed; told me, in so many
words, that I was free to walk in the garden for half an
hour and no longer; and retired, leaving the door open,
that I might avail myself of that permission.

I did so, and did so every morning of my imprisonment, which lasted five days. If I could have seen my
mother alone, I should have gone down on my knees to
her and besought her forgiveness; but I saw no one,
Miss Murdstone excepted, during the while time – except at evening prayers in the parlour; to which I was
escorted by Miss Murdstone after everybody else was
placed; where I was stationed, a young outlaw, all

alone by myself near the door; and whence I was solemnly conducted by my jailer, before any one arose from the devotional posture. I only observed that my mother was as far off from me as she could be, and kept her face another way so that I never saw it; and that Mr Murdstone's hand was bound up in a large linen wrapper.

The length of those five days I can convey no idea of to any one. They occupy the place of years in my remembrance. The way in which I listened to all the incidents of the house that made themselves audible to me; the ringing of bells, the opening and shutting of doors, the murmuring of voices, the footsteps on the stairs; to any laughing, whistling, or singing, outside, which seemed more dismal than anything else to me in my solitude and disgrace – the uncertain pace of the hours, especially at night, when I would wake thinking it was morning, and find that the family were not yet gone to bed, and that all the length of night had yet to come – the depressed dreams and nightmares I had – the return of day, noon, afternoon, evening, when the boys played in the churchyard, and I watched them from a distance within the room, being ashamed to show myself at the window lest they should know I was a prisoner – the strange sensation of never hearing myself speak – the fleeting intervals of something like cheerfulness, which came with eating and drinking, and went away with it – the setting in of rain, one evening, with a fresh smell, and its coming down faster and faster between me and the church, until it and gathering night seemed to quench me in gloom, and fear, and remorse – all this is vividly and strongly stamped on my remembrance.

David Copperfield

Wackford Squeers: Headmaster of Dotheboys Hall

Nicholas Nickleby finds himself recruited as teacher to Dotheboys Hall, a boarding school run by Mr Squeers. Mr Squeers manages the school on the principle that cost must be avoided and that scholarship is an idle luxury, less important than practical experience which can be gained by doing jobs around the Hall.

'Past seven, Nickleby,' said Mr Squeers.

'Has morning come already?' asked Nicholas, sitting up in bed.

'Ah! that has it,' replied Squeers, 'and ready iced too. Now, Nickleby, come; tumble up, will you?'

Nicholas needed no further **admonition**, but 'tumbled up' at once, and proceeded to dress himself by the light of the **taper** which Mr Squeers carried in his hand.

'Here's a pretty go,' said that gentleman; 'the pump's froze.'

'Indeed!' said Nicholas, not much interested.

'Yes,' replied Squeers. 'You can't wash yourself this morning.'

'Not wash myself!' exclaimed Nicholas.

'No, not a bit of it,' rejoined Squeers tartly. 'So you must be content with giving yourself a dry polish till we break the ice in the well, and can get a bucketful out for the boys. Don't stand staring at me, but do look sharp, will you?'

Offering no further observation, Nicholas huddled on his clothes, and Squeers meanwhile opened the shutters and blew the candle out.

'But come,' said Squeers, 'let's go to the school-room', and arming himself with his cane, led the way across a yard to a door in the rear of the house.

'There,' said the schoolmaster as they stepped in to-gether; 'this is our shop, Nickleby.'

It was such a crowded scene, and there were so many objects to attract attention, that at first Nicholas stared about him, really without seeing anything at all. By degrees, however, the place resolved itself into a bare and dirty room with a couple of windows, whereof a tenth part might be of glass, the remainder being stopped up with old copy-books and paper. There were a couple of long old rickety desks, cut and notched, and inked and damaged, in every possible way; two or three forms, a detached desk for Squeers, and another for his assistant. The ceiling was sup-ported like that of a barn, by cross beams and rafters, and the walls were so stained and discoloured, that it was impossible to tell whether they had ever been touched with paint or whitewash.

But the pupils – the young noblemen! The last faint traces of hope, the remotest glimmering of any good to be derived from his efforts in this den, faded from the mind of Nicholas as he looked in dismay around! Pale and haggard faces, lank and bony figures, children with the **countenances** of old men, deformities with

┌ Glossary ─────────────────

admonition: advice, warning
taper: long, very thin candle
countenances: faces, facial expressions

The Internal Economy of Dotheboys Hall

irons upon their limbs, boys of stunted growth, and others whose long **meagre** legs would hardly bear their stooping bodies, all crowded on the view together; there were the bleared eye, the hare-lip, the crooked foot, and every ugliness or distortion that told of unnatural **aversion** conceived by parents for their offspring, or of young lives which, from the earliest dawn of infancy, had been one horrible endurance of cruelty and neglect. There were little faces which should have been handsome, darkened with the scowl of sullen suffering; there was childhood with the light of its eye quenched, its beauty gone, and its helplessness alone remaining; there were vicious-faced boys brooding, with leaden eyes, like **malefactors** in a jail; and there were young creatures on whom the sins of their frail parents had descended, weeping even for the mercenary nurses they had known, and lonesome even in their loneliness. With every kindly sympathy and affection blasted in its birth, with every young and healthy feeling flogged and starved down, with every revengeful passion that can fester in swollen hearts, eating its evil way to their core in silence, what an **incipient** Hell was breeding there!

He could not but observe how silent and sad the boys all seemed to be. There was none of the noise and clamour of a schoolroom, none of its boisterous play or hearty mirth. The children sat crouching and shiver-

---

Glossary

meagre: thin
aversion: strong dislike
malefactors: wrongdoers, criminals
incipient: at an early stage

ing together, and seemed to lack the spirit to move about. The only pupil who **evinced** the slightest tendency towards playfulness was Master Squeers, and as his chief amusement was to tread upon the other boys' toes in his new boots, his flow of spirits was rather disagreeable than otherwise.

After some half-hour's delay Mr Squeers reappeared, and the boys took their places and their books, of which **latter commodity** the average might be about one to eight learners. A few minutes having elapsed, during which Mr Squeers looked very profound, as if he had a **perfect apprehension** of what was inside all the books, and could say every word of their contents by heart if he only chose to take the trouble, that gentleman called up the first class.

Obedient to this summons there ranged themselves in front of the schoolmaster's desk half a dozen scarecrows, out at knees and elbows, one of whom placed a torn and filthy book beneath his learned eye.

'This is the first class in English spelling and philosophy, Nickleby,' said Squeers, beckoning Nicholas to stand beside him. 'Now, then, where's the first boy?'

'Please, sir, he's cleaning the back parlour window,' said the temporary head of the philosophical class.

'So he is, to be sure,' rejoined Squeers. 'We go upon the practical mode of teaching, Nickleby; the regular education system. C-l-e-a-n, clean, verb active, to make bright, to scour. W-i-n, win, d-e-r, der, winder, a casement. When the boy knows this out of book, he goes and does it. Where's the second boy?'

'Please, sir, he's weeding the garden,' replied a small voice.

'To be sure,' said Squeers, by no means disconcerted. 'So he is. B-o-t, bot, t-i-n, tin, bottin, n-e-y, ney, bottinney, noun substantive, a knowledge of plants.

When he has learned that bottinney means a knowledge of plants, he goes and knows 'em. That's our system, Nickleby: what do you think of it?'

'It's a very useful one, at any rate,' answered Nicholas significantly.

'I believe you,' rejoiced Squeers, not **remarking** the emphasis of his **usher**. 'Third boy, what's a horse?'

'A beast, sir,' replied the boy.

'So it is,' said Squeers. 'Ain't it, Nickleby?'

'I believe there is no doubt of that, sir,' answered Nicholas.

'Of course there isn't,' said Squeers. 'A horse is a **quadruped**, and quadruped's Latin for beast, as everybody that's gone through the grammar knows, or else where's the use of having grammars at all?'

'Where, indeed!' said Nicholas abstractedly.

'As you're perfect in that,' resumed Squeers, turning to the boy, 'go and look after *my* horse, and rub him down well, or I'll rub you down. The rest of the class go and draw water up till somebody tells you to leave off, for it's washing day tomorrow, and they want the coppers filled.'

So saying he dismissed the first class to their experiments in practical philosophy, and eyed Nicholas with

┌ Glossary ─

envinced: showed

latter commodity: (here) the books

perfect apprehension: complete knowledge and understanding

remarking: noticing

usher: junior master (often unqualified) in a school

quadruped: four-footed animal

a look half cunning and half doubtful, as if he were not altogether certain what he might think of him by this time.

'That's the way we do it, Nickleby,' he said, after a long pause.

Nicholas shrugged his shoulders in a manner that was scarcely perceptible, and said he saw it was.

There was a small stove at that corner of the room which was nearest to the master's desk, and by it Nicholas sat down, so depressed and self-degraded by the consciousness of his position, that if death could have come upon him at that time he would have been almost happy to meet it. The cruelty of which he had been an unwilling witness, the coarse and ruffianly behaviour of Squeers even in his best moods, the filthy place, the sights and sounds about him, all contributed to this state of feeling; but when he recollected that being there as an assistant, he actually seemed – no matter what unhappy train of circumstances had led him to that pass – to be the **aider and abettor** of a system which filled him with honest disgust and indignation, he loathed himself, and felt for the moment as though the mere consciousness of his present situation must, through all time to come, prevent his raising his head in society again.

Nicholas Nickleby

Glossary

aider and abettor: someone who helps another person to commit a crime

3
Earning an honest living

Dickens' childhood gave him experience of people in a range of trades and crafts. His father, a navy pay clerk, used to take him with him around the docks and riverside, where he noticed the skills and habits of speech of the people who worked there. Later, when his father was sent to a debtors' prison, he met people from the criminal and luckless parts of society – as well as those who made a living from the law and prisons. As a young reporter on a London paper, he also met people who were wealthy, respected and influential.

By his early twenties he had a vast knowledge of the drawing rooms, backstreets, offices and trades of London. He saw the public image of a wealthy city at the heart of the Empire, proud of its civilized institutions of religion, law, industry and commerce. And he also saw the undignified, private life of the city – people working hard to support the whole system and being rewarded with just enough to live on. He was not taken in by appearances, or accents or manners. In his novels, rich or poor are equally likely to be foolish or decent. He shows honour and decency among criminals, and dishonour among the educated and respectable.

Fagin's Academy of Pocket-picking Arts and Sciences

Oliver Twist is having his first experience of life in London. He has been befriended by The Artful Dodger, who offers him a place to sleep. Oliver is very grateful, even if the place is dirty and the behaviour of other boys there is very strange. After his first night he begins to take part in some of the house activities, though, in his innocence, he does not understand what is going on – or what to make of the old gentleman, Fagin, who runs the place.

It was late next morning when Oliver awoke from a sound, long sleep. There was no other person in the room but old Fagin, who was boiling some coffee in a saucepan for breakfast, and whistling softly to himself as he stirred it round and round, with an iron spoon. He would stop every now and then to listen when there was the least noise below; and when he had satisfied himself, he would go on, whistling and stirring again, as before.

Although Oliver had roused himself from sleep, he was not thoroughly awake. There is a drowsy state, between sleeping and waking, when you dream more in five minutes with your eyes half open, and yourself half conscious of everything that is passing around you, than you would in five nights with your eyes fast closed.

Oliver was precisely in this condition. He saw Fagin with his half-closed eyes; heard his low whistling; and recognized the sound of the spoon grating against the saucepan's sides.

When the coffee was done, Fagin drew the saucepan to the hob. Standing, then, for a few minutes, as if he did not well know how to employ himself, he turned round and looked at Oliver, and called him by his name. He did not answer, and was to all appearance asleep.

After satisfying himself upon this, Fagin stepped gently to the door: which he fastened. He then drew forth from some trap in the floor: a small box, which he placed carefully on the table. His eyes glistened as he raised the lid, and looked in. Dragging an old chair to the table, he sat down; and took from it a magnificent gold watch, sparkling with jewels.

'Aha!' said Fagin, shrugging up his shoulders, and distorting every feature with a hideous grin. 'Clever dogs! Clever dogs! Staunch to the last! Never told the old parson where they were. Never **peached** upon old Fagin! And why should they? It wouldn't have loosened **the knot,** or kept **the drop** up, a minute longer. No, no, no! Fine fellows! Fine fellows!'

With these, and other muttered reflections, Fagin once more deposited the watch in its place of safety. At least half a dozen more were drawn forth from the same box, and surveyed with equal pleasure; besides rings, brooches, bracelets, and other articles of jewellery, of such magnificent materials, and costly workmanship, that Oliver had no idea, even of their names.

Glossary

peached: informed, as in criminal 'grassing' or 'squealing'
the knot/the drop: the noose and trap door, features of
  execution by hanging

'What a fine thing capital punishment is! Dead men never repent; dead men never bring awkward stories to light. Ah, it's a fine thing for the trade! Five of 'em strung up in a row, and none left to **play booty**, or turn **white-livered**!'

As Fagin uttered these words, his bright dark eyes, which had been staring vacantly before him, fell on Oliver's face: the boy's eyes were fixed on his in mute curiosity; and although the recognition was only for an instant, it was enough to show the old man that he had been observed. He closed the lid of the box with a loud crash; and, laying his hand on a bread knife which was on the table, started furiously up. He trembled very much though; for, even in his terror, Oliver could see that the knife quivered in the air.

'What's that?' said Fagin. 'What do you watch me for? Why are you awake? What have you seen? Speak out, boy! Quick – quick! for your life!'

'I wasn't able to sleep any longer, sir,' replied Oliver, meekly. 'I am very sorry if I have disturbed you, sir.'

'You were not awake an hour ago?' said Fagin, scowling fiercely on the boy.

'No! No, indeed!' replied Oliver.

'Are you sure?' cried Fagin with a still fiercer look than before: and a threatening attitude.

'Upon my word I was not, sir,' replied Oliver, earnestly. 'I was not, indeed, sir.'

'Tush, tush, my dear!' said Fagin, abruptly resuming his old manner, and playing with the knife a little, before he laid it down; as if to **induce** the belief that he had caught it up, in mere sport. 'Of course I know that, my dear. I only tried to frighten you. You're a brave boy. Ha! ha! you're a brave boy, Oliver!' Fagin rubbed his hands with a chuckle, but glanced uneasily at the box.

'Did you see any of these pretty things, my dear?' said Fagin, laying his hand upon it after a short pause.

'Yes, sir,' replied Oliver.

'Ah!' said Fagin, turning rather pale. 'They – they're mine, Oliver; my little property. All I have to live upon, in my old age. The folks call me a miser, my dear. Only a miser; that's all.'

Oliver thought the old gentleman must be a decided miser to live in such a dirty place, with so many watches; but, thinking that perhaps his fondness for the Dodger and the other boys cost him a good deal of money, he only cast a **deferential** look at Fagin, and asked if he might get up.

'Certainly, my dear, certainly,' replied the old gentleman. 'Stay. There's a pitcher of water in the corner by the door. Bring it here; and I'll give you a basin to wash in, my dear.'

Oliver got up; walked across the room; and stooped for an instant to raise the pitcher. When he turned his head, the box was gone.

He had scarcely washed himself, and made everything tidy, by emptying the basin out of the window, agreeably to Fagin's directions, when the Dodger returned: accompanied by a very sprightly young friend, whom Oliver had seen smoking on the previous night, and who was now formally introduced to him as Charley Bates. The four sat down, to breakfast on the coffee

---

Glossary

play booty: play falsely or gang up to gain something

white-livered: cowardly

induce: encourage, persuade

deferential: polite and respectful

and some hot rolls and ham which the Dodger had brought home in the crown of his hat.

'Well,' said Fagin, glancing slyly at Oliver, and addressing himself to the Dodger, 'I hope you've been at work this morning, my dears?'

'Hard,' replied the Dodger.

'As nails,' added Charley Bates.

'Good boys, good boys!' said Fagin. 'What have *you* got, Dodger?'

'A couple of pocket-books,' replied that young gentleman.

'Lined?' inquired Fagin, with eagerness.

'Pretty well,' replied the Dodger, producing two pocket-books; one green, and the other red.

'Not so heavy as they might be,' said Fagin, after looking at the insides carefully; 'but very neat and nicely made. **Ingenious** workman, ain't he, Oliver?'

'Very, indeed, sir,' said Oliver. At which Mr Charles Bates laughed uproariously; very much to the amazement of Oliver, who saw nothing to laugh at, in anything that had passed.

'And what have you got, my dear?' said Fagin to Charley Bates.

'Wipes,' replied Master Bates; at the same time producing four pocket-handkerchiefs.

'Well,' said Fagin, inspecting them closely; 'they're very good ones, very. You haven't marked them well, though, Charley; so the marks shall be picked out with a needle, and we'll teach Oliver how to do it. Shall us, Oliver, eh? Ha! ha! ha!'

'If you please, sir,' said Oliver.

'You'd like to be able to make pocket-handkerchiefs as easy as Charley Bates, wouldn't you, my dear?' said Fagin.

'Very much, indeed, if you'll teach me, sir,' replied Oliver.

Master Bates saw something so **exquisitely ludicrous** in this reply that he burst into another laugh; which laugh, meeting the coffee he was drinking, and carrying it down some wrong channel, very nearly terminated in his premature suffocation.

'He is so jolly **green**!' said Charley when he recovered, as an apology to the company for his unpolite behaviour.

The Dodger said nothing, but he smoothed Oliver's hair over his eyes, and said he'd know better, by-and-bye; upon which the old gentleman, observing Oliver's colour mounting, changed the subject by asking whether there had been much of a crowd at the execution that morning? This made him wonder more and more; for it was plain from the replies of the two boys that they had both been there; and Oliver naturally wondered how they could possibly have found time to be so very **industrious**.

When the breakfast was cleared away, the merry old gentleman and the two boys played at a very curious and uncommon game, which was performed in this way. The merry old gentleman, placing a snuff-box in one pocket of his trousers, a note-case in the other, and a watch in his waistcoat pocket, with a guard-chain

---

Glossary

ingenious: inventive and clever
exquisitely ludicrous: perfectly ridiculous
green: naïve, innocent
industrious: hard-working

round his neck, and sticking a mock diamond pin in his shirt: buttoned his coat tight round him, and putting his spectacle case and handkerchief in his pockets, trotted up and down the room with a stick, in imitation of the manner in which old gentlemen walk about the streets any hour in the day. Sometimes he stopped at the fireplace, and sometimes at the door, making believe that he was staring with all his might into shop-windows. At such times he would look constantly round him, for fear of thieves, and would keep slapping all his pockets in turn, to see that he hadn't lost anything, in such a very funny and natural manner, that Oliver laughed till the tears ran down his face. All this time, the two boys followed him closely about, getting out of his sight, so nimbly, every time he turned round, that it was impossible to follow their motions. At last, the Dodger trod upon his toes, or ran upon his boot accidentally, while Charley Bates stumbled up against him behind; and in that one moment they took from him, with the most extraordinary rapidity, snuff-box, note-case, watch-guard, chain, shirt-pin, pocket-hand-kerchief, – even the spectacle case. If the old gentleman felt a hand in any one of his pockets, he cried out where it was; and then the game began all over again.

When this game had been played a great many times, a couple of young ladies called to see the young gentlemen; one of whom was named Bet, and the other Nancy. They wore a good deal of hair, not very neatly turned up behind, and were rather untidy about the shoes and stockings. They were not exactly pretty, perhaps; but they had a great deal of colour in their faces, and looked quite stout and hearty. Being remarkably free and agreeable in their manners, Oliver thought them very nice girls indeed. As there is no doubt they were.

Oliver's reception by Fagin and the boys

These visitors stopped a long time. Spirits were produced, **in consequence of** one of the young ladies complaining of a coldness in her inside; and the conversation took a very **convivial** and improving turn. At length, Charley Bates expressed his opinion that it was time to pad the hoof. This, it occurred to Oliver, must be French for going out; for, directly afterwards, the Dodger, and Charley, and the two young ladies, went away together, having been kindly **furnished** by the amiable old gentleman with money to spend.

'There, my dear,' said Fagin. 'That's a pleasant life, isn't it? They have gone out for the day.'

'Have they done work, sir?' inquired Oliver.

'Yes,' said Fagin; 'that is, unless they should unexpectedly come across any, when they are out; and they won't neglect it, if they do, my dear, depend upon it. Make 'em your models, my dear. Make 'em your models,' tapping the fire-shovel on the hearth to add force to his words; 'do everything they bid you, and take their advice in all matters – especially the Dodger's, my dear. He'll be a great man himself, and will make you one too, if you take pattern by him – Is my handkerchief hanging out of my pocket, my dear?' said Fagin, stopping short.

'Yes, sir,' said Oliver.

'See if you can take it out, without my feeling it: as you saw them do, when we were at play this morning.'

Oliver held up the bottom of the pocket with one hand, as he had seen the Dodger hold it, and drew the handkerchief lightly out of it with the other.

'Is it gone?' cried the Jew.

'Here it is, sir,' said Oliver, showing it in his hand.

'You're a clever boy, my dear,' said the playful old gentleman, patting Oliver on the head approvingly. 'I never saw a sharper lad. Here's a shilling for you. If you go on, in this way, you'll be the greatest man of the time. And now come here, and I'll show you how to take the marks out of the handkerchiefs.'

Oliver wondered what picking the old gentleman's pocket in play had to do with his chances of being a great man. But, thinking that Fagin, being so much his senior, must know best, he followed him quietly to the table, and was soon deeply involved in his new study.

For many days, Oliver remained in Fagin's room, picking the marks out of the pocket-handkerchiefs (of which a great number were brought home) and sometimes taking part in the game already described: which the two boys and Fagin played, regularly, every morning. At length, he began to **languish** for fresh air, and took many occasions of earnestly **entreating** the old gentleman to allow him to go out to work, with his two companions.

Oliver was **rendered** the more anxious to be actively employed, by what he had seen of the stern morality of the old gentleman's character. Whenever the Dodger or Charley Bates came home at night, empty-handed, he would **expatiate** with great **vehemence** on the

Glossary

in consequence of: because of, as a result of

convivial: sociable and cheerful

furnished: provided

languish: to droop and pine

entreating: begging

rendered: made

expatiate: talk at length

vehemence: force and urgency

misery of idle and lazy habits; and would enforce upon them the necessity of an active life, by sending them supperless to bed. On one occasion, indeed, he even went so far as to knock them both down a flight of stairs; but this was carrying out his **virtuous precepts** to an unusual extent.

Oliver Twist

Glossary

virtuous precepts: moral teachings

Being jolly under circumstances: Mark Tapley

Mark Tapley is happy in his work at the Blue Dragon, where his good nature makes him popular with all. However, he wants to know if he's 'jolly' because he's got a cheerful job in a cheerful place to work, or whether he's 'jolly' by nature and would be the same wherever he worked and whatever he did. He decides that the only way to find out is to leave his job and test himself in an uncheerful job, where there would be 'more credit in being jolly'.

Mark Tapley did not hear the sound of wheels until it was close behind him; when he turned a **whimsical** face and a very merry pair of blue eyes on Mr Pinch, and **checked himself** directly.

'Why, Mark!' said Tom Pinch, stopping. 'Who'd have thought of seeing you here? Well! this is surprising!'

Mark touched his hat, and said, with a very sudden decrease of **vivacity**, that he was going to Salisbury.

'And how **spruce** you are, too!' said Mr Pinch, surveying him with great pleasure. 'Really, I didn't think you were half such a tight-made fellow, Mark!'

Glossary

whimsical: humorous
checked himself: stopped
vivacity: liveliness
spruce: smart

'Thankee, Mr Pinch. Pretty well for that, I believe. It's not my fault, you know. With regard to being spruce, sir, that's where it is, you see.' And here he looked particularly gloomy.

'Where what is?' Mr Pinch demanded.

'Where the **aggravation** of it is. Any man may be in good spirits and good temper when he's well dressed. There ain't much credit in that. If I was very ragged and very jolly, then I should begin to feel I had gained a point, Mr Pinch.'

'So you were singing just now, to bear up, as it were, against being well dressed, eh, Mark?' said Pinch.

'Your conversation's always equal to print, sir,' rejoined Mark, with a broad grin. 'That was it.'

'Well!' cried Pinch, 'you are the strangest young man, Mark, I ever knew in my life. I always thought so; but now I am quite certain of it. I am going to Salisbury, too. Will you get in? I shall be very glad of your company.'

The young fellow made his acknowledgements and accepted the offer; stepping into the carriage directly, and seating himself on the very edge of the seat with his body half out of it, to express his being there on sufferance, and by the politeness of Mr Pinch. As they went along, the conversation proceeded after this manner.

'I more than half believed, just now, seeing you so very smart,' said Pinch, 'that you must be going to be married, Mark.'

'Well, sir, I've thought of that, too,' he replied. 'There might be some credit in being jolly with a wife, 'specially if the children had the measles and that, and was very **fractious** indeed. But I'm a'most afraid to try it. I don't see my way clear.'

'You're not very fond of anybody, perhaps?' said Pinch.

'Not particular, sir, I think.'

'But the way would be, you know, Mark, according to your views of things,' said Mr Pinch, 'to marry somebody you didn't like, and who was very disagreeable.'

'So it would, sir; but that might be carrying out a principle a little too far, mightn't it?'

'Perhaps it might,' said Mr Pinch. At which they both laughed gaily.

'Lord bless you, sir,' said Mark, 'you don't half know me, though. I don't believe there ever was a man as could come out so strong under circumstances that would make other men miserable, as I could, if I could only get a chance. But I can't get a chance. It's my opinion that nobody never will know half of what's in me, unless something very unexpected turns up. And I don't see any prospect of that. I'm a-going to leave the Dragon, sir.'

'Going to leave the Dragon!' cried Mr Pinch, looking at him with great astonishment. 'Why, Mark, you take my breath away!'

'Yes, sir,' he rejoined, looking straight before him and a long way off, as men do sometimes when they **cogitate profoundly**. 'What's the use of my stopping at the Dragon? It ain't at all the sort of place for *me*. When I left London (I'm a Kentish man by birth,

---

Glossary

aggravation: annoyance
fractious: irritable and difficult
cogitate profoundly: think deeply

though), and took that situation here, I quite made up my mind that it was the dullest little out-of-the-way corner in England, and that there would be some credit in being jolly under such circumstances. But, Lord, there's no dullness at the Dragon! Skittles, cricket, **quoits**, nine-pins, comic songs, choruses, company round the chimney corner every winter's evening. Any man could be jolly at the Dragon. There's no credit in *that*.'

'But if **common report** be true for once, Mark, as I think it is, being able to confirm it by what I know myself,' said Mr Pinch, 'you are the cause of half this merriment, and set it going.'

'There may be something in that, too, sir,' answered Mark. 'But that's no consolation.'

'Well!' said Mr Pinch, after a short silence, his usually subdued tone being even more subdued than ever. 'I can hardly think enough of what you tell me. Why, what will become of Mrs Lupin, Mark?'

Mark looked more fixedly before him, and further off still, as he answered that he didn't suppose it would be much of an object to her. There were plenty of smart young fellows as would be glad of the place. He knew a dozen himself.

'That's probable enough,' said Mr Pinch, 'but I am not at all sure that Mrs Lupin would be glad of them. Why, I always supposed that Mrs Lupin and you would make a match of it, Mark: and so did every one, as far as I know.'

'I never,' Mark replied, in some confusion, 'said nothing as was in a direct way courting-like to her, nor she to me, but I don't know what I mightn't do one of these odd times, and what she mightn't say in answer. Well, sir, *that* wouldn't suit.'

'Not to be landlord of the Dragon, Mark?' cried Mr Pinch.

'No, sir, certainly not,' returned the other, withdrawing his gaze from the horizon, and looking at his fellow traveller. 'Why, that would be the ruin of a man like me. I go and sit down comfortably for life, and no man never finds me out. What would be the credit of the landlord of the Dragon's being jolly? Why, he couldn't help it, if he tried.'

'Does Mrs Lupin know you are going to leave her?' Mr Pinch inquired.

'I haven't broke it to her yet, sir, but I must. I'm looking out this morning for something new and suitable,' he said, nodding towards the city.

'What kind of thing, now?' Mr Pinch demanded.

'I was thinking,' Mark replied, 'of something in the grave-digging way.'

'Good gracious, Mark!' cried Mr Pinch.

'It's a good damp, wormy sort of business, sir,' said Mark, shaking his head argumentatively, 'and there might be some credit in being jolly, with one's mind in that pursuit, unless grave-diggers is usually given that way; which would be a drawback. You don't happen to know, do you, sir?'

'No,' said Mr Pinch, 'I don't indeed. I never thought upon the subject.'

'In case of that not turning out as well as one could wish, you know,' said Mark, musing again, 'there's

Glossary

quoits: team game involving the throwing of heavy metal rings at a post set in the ground

common report: gossip, the talk of the town

other businesses. Undertaking now. That's gloomy. There might be credit to be gained there. A broker's man in a poor neighbourhood wouldn't be bad perhaps. A jailor sees a deal of misery. A doctor's man is in the very midst of murder. A bailiff's an't a lively office nat'rally. Even a tax-gatherer must find his feelings rather worked upon, at times. There's lots of trades in which I should have an opportunity, I think.'

Mr Pinch was so perfectly overwhelmed by these remarks that he could do nothing but occasionally exchange a word or two on some indifferent subject, and cast sidelong glances at the bright face of his odd friend (who seemed quite unconscious of his observation), until they reached a certain corner of the road, close upon the outskirts of the city, when Mark said he would jump down there, if he pleased.

'But bless my soul, Mark,' said Mr Pinch, who in the progress of his observation just then made the discovery that the bosom of his companion's shirt was as much exposed as if it was Midsummer, and was ruffled by every breath of air, 'why don't you wear a waistcoat?'

'What's the good of one, sir?' asked Mark.

'Good of one?' said Mr Pinch. 'Why, to keep your chest warm.'

'Lord love you, sir!' cried Mark, 'you don't know me. *My* chest don't want no warming. Even if it did, what would no waistcoat bring it to? Inflammation of the lungs, perhaps? Well, there'd be some credit in being jolly, with a inflammation of the lungs.'

As Mr Pinch returned no other answer than such as was conveyed in his breathing very hard, and opening his eyes very wide, and nodding his head very much, Mark thanked him for his ride, and without troubling him to stop, jumped lightly down. And away he fluttered, with his red neckerchief, and his open coat, down a cross-lane: turning back from time to time to nod to Mr Pinch, and looking one of the most careless, good-humoured, comical fellows in life. His late companion, with a thoughtful face, pursued his way to Salisbury.

Martin Chuzzlewit

4
Romantic pursuits

Romantic fiction was popular with readers in Dickens' day, but relations between the sexes in his novels are not quite as happy and romantic as some readers would like. Some of his partners in love are affectionate and happy, but others show how marriage can be a cruel trap, more to do with parents' wishes or money than with love. Dickens was aware that for many women in his time, the only way to make sure of a stable economic future was to marry a wealthy man. Loveless marriages feature in several of his novels, and he makes the reader see the results of being trapped in marriage to a partner lacking understanding and warmth. However, Dickens' sense of humour shows itself in this as in other matters, and he balances the serious with a comic view of marriage as a war between the sexes, represented by equally unattractive partners. Mr and Mrs Bumble are a good example of this.

Dickens was careful not to offend his readers by criticizing marriage in general, but some of his pairings draw attention to the less romantic aspects of holy matrimony. At the time Dickens was writing, the Church and the Royal Family promoted marriage and family life as foundations of sound moral values. Dickens was not willing to create a public debate about the issue, but made it his business to show how the reality may be less than the ideal, especially choosing wealthy, respectable members of society to show how the family could be as much a prison as a promise of bliss.

Broken-hearted vengeance: Miss Havisham

Pip, the adopted child of his sister and her blacksmith husband, Joe Gargery, is invited to Satis House where he discovers the proud young Estella (also an adopted child) and Miss Havisham. She has kept everything in the house exactly as it was on the morning, years ago, when she was to be married: the remains of the wedding cake are still on the table, cobwebbed and mouse-eaten, the clocks are stopped and she is still in her wedding dress. Bitter and heart-broken as a result of being jilted on her wedding day, she makes Estella cold and cruel to young Pip as part of her revenge on men.

I found myself in a pretty large room, well lighted with wax candles. No glimpse of daylight was to be seen in it. It was a dressing-room, as I supposed from the furniture, though much of it was of forms and uses then quite unknown to me. But prominent in it was a draped table with a gilded looking-glass, and that I made out at first sight to be a fine lady's dressing-table.

In an armchair, with an elbow resting on the table and her head leaning on that hand, sat the strangest lady I have ever seen, or shall ever see.

She was dressed in rich materials – satins, and lace, and silks – all of white. Her shoes were white. And she had a long white veil dependent from her hair, and she had bridal flowers in her hair, but her hair was white. Some bright jewels sparkled on her neck and on her hands, and some other jewels lay sparkling on the

Miss Havisham

table. Dresses, less splendid than the dress she wore, and half-packed trunks, were scattered about. She had not quite finished dressing, for she had **but** one shoe on – the other was on the table near her hand – her veil was but half arranged, her watch and chain were not put on, and some lace for her bosom lay with those trinkets, and with her handkerchief, and gloves, and some flowers, and a Prayer Book, all confusedly heaped about the looking-glass.

It was not in the first moments that I saw all these things, though I saw more of them in the first moments than might be supposed. But I saw that everything within my view which ought to be white, and had been white long ago, had lost its lustre, and was faded and yellow. I saw that the bride within the bridal dress had withered like the dress, and like the flowers, and had no brightness left but the brightness of her sunken eyes. I saw that the dress had been put upon the rounded figure of a young woman, and that the figure upon which it now hung loose, had shrunk to skin and bone. Once, I had been taken to see some ghastly waxworks at the Fair. Once, I had been taken to one of our old marsh churches to see a skeleton in the ashes of a rich dress, that had been dug out of a vault under the Church pavement. Now, waxwork and skeleton seemed to have dark eyes that moved and looked at me. I should have cried out, if I could.

'Who is it?' said the lady at the table.

'Pip, ma'am.'

'Pip?'

'Mr Pumblechook's boy, ma'am. Come – to play.'

'Come nearer; let me look at you. Come close.'

It was when I stood before her, avoiding her eyes, that I took note of the surrounding objects in detail, and saw that her watch had stopped at twenty minutes to nine, and that a clock in the room had stopped at twenty minutes to nine.

'Look at me,' said Miss Havisham. 'You are not afraid of a woman who has never seen the sun since you were born?'

I regret to state that I was not afraid of telling the enormous lie **comprehended** in the answer, 'No.'

'Do you know what I touch here?' she said, laying her hands, one upon the other, on her left side.

'Yes, ma'am.'

'What do I touch?'

'Your heart.'

'Broken!'

She uttered the word with an eager look, and with strong emphasis, and with a weird smile that had a kind of boast in it. Afterwards, she kept her hands there for a little while, and slowly took them away as if they were heavy.

'I am tired,' said Miss Havisham. 'I want **diversion**, and I have done with men and women. Play.'

I think it will be conceded by my most **disputatious** reader, that she could hardly have directed an unfortunate boy to do anything in the wide world more difficult to be done under the circumstances.

'I sometimes have sick fancies,' she went on, 'and I have a sick fancy that I want to see some play. There,

Glossary

but: only

comprehended: involved, incorporated

diversion: amusement, distraction

disputatious: argumentative

there!' with an impatient movement of the fingers of her right hand; 'play, play, play!'

I felt myself so **unequal to** performance that I stood looking at Miss Havisham in what I suppose she took for a dogged manner, inasmuch as she said, when we had taken a good look at each other –

'Are you sullen and obstinate?'

'No, ma'am, I am very sorry for you, and very sorry I can't play just now. If you complain of me I shall get into trouble, so I would do it if I could; but it's so new here, and so strange, and so fine – and melancholy – ' I stopped, fearing I might say too much, or had already said it, and we took another look at each other.

Before she spoke again, she turned her eyes from me, and looked at the dress she wore, and at the dressing-table, and finally at herself in the looking-glass.

'So new to him,' she muttered, 'so old to me; so strange to him, so familiar to me; so melancholy to both of us! Call Estella.'

As she was still looking at the reflection of herself, I thought she was still talking to herself, and kept quiet.

'Call Estella,' she repeated, flashing a look at me. 'You can do that. Call Estella. At the door.'

To stand in the dark in a mysterious passage of an unknown house, bawling Estella to a scornful young lady neither visible nor responsive, and feeling it a dreadful liberty so to roar out her name, was almost as bad as playing to order. But she answered at last, and her light came along the dark passage like a star.

Miss Havisham beckoned her to come close, and took up a jewel from the table, and tried its effect upon her fair young bosom and against her pretty brown hair. 'Your own, one day, my dear, and you will use it well. Let me see you play cards with this boy.'

'With this boy! Why, he is a common labouring-boy!'

I thought I overheard Miss Havisham answer – only it seemed so unlikely – 'Well! You can break his heart.'

'What do you play, boy?' asked Estella of myself with the greatest **disdain**.

'Nothing but **beggar my neighbour**, miss.'

'Beggar him,' said Miss Havisham to Estella. So we sat down to cards.

It was then I began to understand that everything in the room had stopped, like the watch and the clock, a long time ago. I noticed that Miss Havisham put down the jewel exactly on the spot from which she had taken it up. As Estella dealt the cards, I glanced at the dressing-table again, and saw that the shoe upon it, once white, now yellow, had never been worn. I glanced down at the foot from which the shoe was absent, and saw that the silk stocking on it, once white, now yellow, had been trodden ragged. Without this arrest of everything, this standing still of all the pale decayed objects, not even the withered bridal dress on the collapsed form could have looked so like grave-clothes, or the long veil so like a shroud.

So she sat, corpse-like, as we played at cards; the frillings and trimmings on her bridal dress looking like earthy paper. I knew nothing then of the discoveries that are occasionally made of bodies buried in ancient times, which fall to powder in the moment of being distinctly seen; but I have often thought since, that she

┌Glossary

unequal to: not up to

disdain: scorn, contempt

beggar my neighbour: a card game, the winner being the one who gains all the cards in the pack

must have looked as if the natural light of day would have struck her to dust.

'He calls the knaves, Jacks, this boy!' said Estella with disdain, before our first game was out. 'And what coarse hands he has! And what thick boots!'

I had never thought of being ashamed of my hands before; but I began to consider them a very indifferent pair. Her contempt was so strong, that it became infectious, and I caught it.

She won the game, and I dealt. I misdealt, as was only natural, when I knew she was lying in wait for me to do wrong; and she denounced me for a stupid, clumsy labouring-boy.

'You say nothing of her,' remarked Miss Havisham to me, as she looked on. 'She says many hard things of you, but you say nothing of her. What do you think of her?'

'I don't like to say,' I stammered.

'Tell me in my ear,' said Miss Havisham, bending down.

'I think she is very proud,' I replied in a whisper.

'Anything else?'

'I think she is very pretty,'

'Anything else?'

'I think she is very insulting.' (She was looking at me then, with a look of supreme **aversion**.)

'Anything else?'

'I think I should like to go home.'

'And never see her again, though she is so pretty?'

'I am not sure that I shouldn't like to see her again, but I should like to go home now.'

'You shall go soon,' said Miss Havisham aloud. 'Play the game out.'

Saving for the one weird smile at first, I should have felt almost sure that Miss Havisham's face could not smile. It had dropped into a watchful and brooding expression – most likely when all the things about her had become transfixed – and it looked as if nothing could ever lift it up again. Her chest had dropped, so that she stooped; and her voice had dropped, so that she spoke low, and with a dead lull upon her; altogether, she had the appearance of having dropped, body and soul, within and without, under the weight of a crushing blow.

I played the game to an end with Estella, and she beggared me. She threw the cards down on the table when she had won them all, as if she despised them for having been won of me.

'When shall I have you here again?' said Miss Havisham. 'Let me think.'

I was beginning to remind her that today was Wednesday, when she checked me with her former impatient movement of the fingers of her right hand.

'There, there! I know nothing of days of the week; I know nothing of weeks of the year. Come again after six days. You hear?'

'Yes, ma'am.'

'Estella, take him down. Let him have something to eat, and let him roam and look about him while he eats. Go, Pip.'

I followed the candle down. Until she opened the side entrance, I had fancied, without thinking about it, that it must be night time. The rush of the daylight quite confounded me, and made me feel as if I had been in the candlelight of the strange room many hours.

Glossary

aversion: extreme dislike

'You are to wait here, you boy,' said Estella; and disappeared and closed the door.

I took the opportunity of being alone in the court-yard to look at my coarse hands and my common boots. My opinion of those accessories was not favourable. They had never troubled me before, but they troubled me now, as vulgar appendages. I determined to ask Joe why he had ever taught me to call those picture-cards, Jacks, which ought to be called knaves. I wished Joe had been rather more genteelly brought up, and then I should have been so too.

She came back, with some bread and meat and a little mug of beer. She put the mug down on the stones of the yard, and gave me the bread and meat without looking at me, as insolently as if I were a dog in dis-grace. I was so humiliated, hurt, spurned, offended, angry, sorry – I cannot hit upon the right name for the smart – God knows what its name was – that tears started to my eyes. The moment they sprang there, the girl looked at me with a quick delight in having been the cause of them. This gave me power to keep them back and to look at her: so she gave a contemptuous toss – but with a sense, I thought, of having made too sure that I was so wounded – and left me.

But, when she was gone, I looked about me for a place to hide my face in, and got behind one of the gates in the brewery lane, and leaned my sleeve against the wall there, and leaned my forehead on it, and cried. As I cried, I kicked the wall, and took a hard twist at my hair; so bitter were my feelings, and so sharp was the smart without a name, that needed counteraction.

Great Expectations

Sam Weller writes a Valentine

Sam Weller has romantic feelings for a girl he met in Ipswich, and decides to send her a Valentine. After much exercise of brain, hand and ink, he is proud of the verse he has composed to put in the card. His father, however, thinking of his own experience, is less inclined to see females in a romantic light, and warns his son of the dangers where verse and women are concerned. Despite his warnings, Sam refuses to be put off his romantic gesture.

Mr Weller turned, and began **wending** his way towards Leadenhall Market, through a variety of bye streets and courts. As he was sauntering away his spare time, and stopped to look at almost every object that met his gaze, it is by no means surprising that Mr Weller should have paused before a small stationer's and print-seller's window; but without further explanation it does appear surprising that his eyes should have no sooner rested on certain pictures which were exposed for sale therein, than he gave a sudden start, smote his right leg with great **vehemence**, and exclaimed with energy, 'If it hadn't been for this, I should ha' forgot all about it, till it was too late!'

Glossary

wending: walking slowly
vehemence: forcefulness of speech

The particular picture on which Sam Weller's eyes were fixed, as he said this, was a highly coloured representation of a couple of human hearts skewered together with an arrow, cooking before a cheerful fire, while a male and female cannibal in modern attire: the gentleman being clad in a blue coat and white trousers, and the lady in a deep red **pelisse** with a parasol of the same: were approaching the meal with hungry eyes, up a **serpentine** gravel path leading **thereunto**. A decidedly indelicate young gentleman, in a pair of wings and nothing else, was depicted as superintending the cooking; and the whole formed a 'valentine,' of which, as a written inscription in the window testified, there was a large assortment within, which the shopkeeper pledged himself to dispose of at the reduced rate of one and sixpence each.

'I should ha' forgot it; I should certainly ha' forgot it!' said Sam; so saying, he at once stepped into the stationer's shop, and requested to be served with a sheet of the best gilt-edged letter-paper, and a hard-nibbed pen which could be **warranted** not to splutter. These articles having been promptly supplied, he walked on direct towards Leadenhall Market at a good pace, very different from his recent lingering one. Looking round him, he there beheld a signboard on which the painter's art had **delineated** something remotely resembling a **cerulean** elephant with an **aquiline** nose **in lieu of** trunk. Rightly **conjecturing** that this was the Blue Boar himself, he stepped into the house, and inquired concerning his parent.

'He won't be here this three quarters of an hour or more,' said the young lady who superintended the domestic arrangements of the Blue Boar. 'Very good, my dear,' replied Sam. 'Let me have nine penn'orth o' brandy and water luke, and the inkstand, will you miss?'

The brandy and water luke, and the inkstand, having been carried into the little parlour, and the young lady having carefully flattened down the coals to prevent their blazing, and carried away the poker to preclude the possibility of the fire being stirred, Sam Weller sat himself down in a box near the stove, and pulled out the sheet of gilt-edged letter-paper, and the hard-nibbed pen. Then looking carefully at the pen to see that there were no hairs in it, and dusting down the table, so that there might be no crumbs of bread under the paper, Sam tucked up the cuffs of his coat, squared his elbows, and composed himself to write.

To ladies and gentlemen who are not in the habit of devoting themselves practically to the science of penmanship, writing a letter is no very easy task; it being always considered necessary in such cases for the writer to recline his head on his left arm, so as to place his eyes as nearly as possible on a level with the paper, while glancing sideways at the letters he is constructing, to form with his tongue imaginary characters to

---

┌─ Glossary ─────────────────────

pelisse: child's or woman's long outdoor cloak

serpentine: winding

thereunto: to it, i.e. to the place just mentioned

warranted: guaranteed

delineated: drawn, outlined

cerulean: blue

aquiline: curved or hooked like the beak of an eagle

in lieu of: in place of, instead

conjecturing: assuming, supposing

correspond. These motions, although unquestionably of the greatest assistance to original composition, **retard** in some degree the progress of the writer; and Sam had unconsciously been a full hour and a half writing words in small text, smearing out wrong letters with his little finger, and putting in new ones which required going over very often to render them visible through the old blots, when he was roused by the opening of the door and the entrance of his parent.

'Well, Sammy,' said the father.

'Well,' responded the son, laying down his pen. 'What's the last bulletin about mother-in-law?'

'Mrs Weller passed a very good night, but is uncommon perverse, and unpleasant this mornin'. Signed upon oath, T. Weller, Esquire, Senior. That's the last wun as was issued, Sammy,' replied Mr Weller, untying his shawl.

'No better yet?' inquired Sam.

'All the symptoms aggeravated,' replied Mr Weller, shaking his head. 'But wot's that, you're a doin' of? Pursuit of knowledge under difficulties, Sammy?'

'I've done now,' said Sam with slight embarrassment; 'I've been a writin'.'

'So I see,' replied Mr Weller. 'Not to any young 'ooman, I hope, Sammy?'

'Why it's no use a sayin' it ain't,' replied Sam, 'It's a valentine.'

'A what!' exclaimed Mr Weller, apparently horror-stricken by the word.

'A valentine,' replied Sam.

'Samiwel, Samiwel,' said Mr Weller, in reproachful accents, 'I didn't think you'd ha' done it. Arter the warnin' you've had, arter all I've said to you upon this here very subject; arter activally seein' and bein' in the company o' your own mother-in-law, wich I should ha' thought wos a moral lesson as no man could never ha' forgotten to his dyin' day! I didn't think you'd ha' done it, Sammy, I didn't think you'd ha' done it!' These reflections were too much for the good old man. He raised Sam's tumbler to his lips and drank off its contents.

'Wot's the matter now?' said Sam.

'Nev'r mind, Sammy,' replied Mr Weller, 'it'll be a very agonizin' trial to me at my time of life, but I'm pretty tough, that's wun consolation, as the very old turkey remarked wen the farmer said he wos afeerd he should be obliged to kill him for the London market.'

'Wot'll be a trial?' inquired Sam.

'To see you married, Sammy – to see you a dilluded victim, and thinkin' in your innocence that it's all very capital,' replied Mr Weller. 'It's a dreadful trial to a father's feelin's, that 'ere, Sammy.'

'Nonsense,' said Sam. 'I ain't a goin' to get married, don't you fret yourself about that; I know you're a judge of these things. Order in your pipe, and I'll read you the letter. There!'

We cannot distinctly say whether it was the prospect of the pipe, or the consolatory reflection that a fatal disposition to get married ran in the family and couldn't be helped, which calmed Mr Weller's feelings, and caused his grief to subside. We should be rather disposed to say that the result was attained by combining the two sources of consolation, for he repeated the second in a low tone, very frequently; ringing the bell meanwhile, to order in the first. He then divested him-

Glossary

retard: hold back, slow down

He lit his pipe and placed himself in front of the fire with his back towards it ...

self of his upper coat; and lighting the pipe and placing himself in front of the fire with his back towards it, so that he could feel its full heat, and recline against the mantelpiece at the same time, turned towards Sam, and, with a **countenance** greatly **mollified** by the softening influence of tobacco, requested him to 'fire away.'

Sam dipped his pen into the ink to be ready for any corrections, and began with a very theatrical air:

'"Lovely –."'

'Stop,' said Mr Weller, ringing the bell. 'A double glass o' the **invariable**, my dear.'

'Very well, sir,' replied the girl; who with great quickness appeared, vanished, returned, and disappeared.

'They seem to know your ways here,' observed Sam.

'Yes,' replied his father, 'I've been here before, in my time. Go on, Sammy.'

'"Lovely creetur,"' repeated Sam.

'"Tain't in poetry, is it?' interposed his father.

'No, no,' replied Sam.

'Verry glad to hear it,' said Mr Weller. 'Poetry's unnat'ral; no man ever talked poetry 'cept a **beadle** on boxin' day, or some o' them low fellows; never you let yourself down to talk poetry, my boy. Begin agin, Sammy.'

Glossary

countenance: face, expression

mollified: calmed down, soothed

invariable: 'my usual'

beadle: parish official, a little like a constable

Mr Weller resumed his pipe with critical solemnity, and Sam once more commenced, and read as follows.

'"Lovely creetur I feel myself a dammed" –.'

'That ain't proper,' said Mr Weller, taking his pipe from his mouth.

'No; it ain't "dammed",' observed Sam, holding the letter up to the light, 'it's "shamed," there's a blot there – "I feel myself ashamed."'

'Verry good,' said Mr Weller. 'Go on.'

'"Feel myself ashamed, and completely cir –" I forget what this here word is,' said Sam, scratching his head with the pen, in vain attempts to remember.

'Why don't you look at it, then?' inquired Mr Weller.

'So I *am* a lookin' at it,' replied Sam, 'but there's another blot. Here's a "c," and a "i," and a "d."'

'**Circumvented**, p'haps,' suggested Mr Weller.

'No, it ain't that,' said Sam, '**circumscribed**; that's it.'

'That ain't as good a word as circumvented, Sammy,' said Mr Weller, gravely.

'Think not?' said Sam.

'Nothin' like it,' replied his father.

'But don't you think it means more?' inquired Sam.

'Well p'raps it is a more tenderer word,' said Mr Weller, after a few moments' reflection. 'Go on, Sammy.'

'"Feel myself ashamed and completely circumscribed in a dressin' of you, for you *are* a nice gal and nothin' but it."'

'That's a verry pretty **sentiment**,' said the elder Mr Weller, removing his pipe to make way for the remark.

'Yes, I think it is rayther good,' observed Sam, highly flattered.

'Wot I like in that 'ere style of writin',' said the elder Mr Weller, 'is, that there ain't no callin' names in it, –

no Venuses, nor nothin' o' that kind. Wot's the good o'callin' a young 'ooman a Venus or a angel, Sammy?'

'Ah! what, indeed?' replied Sam.

'You might jist as well call her a **griffin**, or a unicorn, or a king's arms at once, which is verry well known to be a collection o' fabulous animals,' added Mr Weller.

'Just as well,' replied Sam.

'Drive on, Sammy,' said Mr Weller.

Sam complied with the request, and proceeded as follows; his father continuing to smoke, with a mixed expression of wisdom and complacency.

'"Afore I see you, I thought all women was alike."'

'So they are,' observed the elder Mr Weller.

'"But now," continued Sam, "now I find what a reg'lar soft-headed, ink-red'lous turnip I must ha' been; for there ain't nobody like you, though *I* like you better than nothin' at all." I thought it best to make that rayther strong,' said Sam, looking up.

Mr Weller nodded approvingly, and Sam resumed.

'"So I take the privilidge of the day, Mary my dear, to tell you that the first and only time I see you, your likeness was took on my hart in much quicker time and brighter colours than ever a likeness was took by the **profeel macheen** (wich p'raps you may have heerd on Mary my dear) altho it *does* finish a portrait and put

---

Glossary

circumvented: avoided, went round

circumscribed: drew a line around, circled

sentiment: expression of feeling or emotion

griffin: a mythological animal with a lion's body and an eagle's head and wings

profeel macheen: simple kind of camera which made a silhouette or profile of a person's face

the frame and glass on complete, with a hook at the end to hang it up by, and all in two minutes and a quarter."'

'I am afeerd that verges on the poetical, Sammy,' said Mr Weller, dubiously.

'No it don't,' replied Sam, reading on very quickly, to avoid contesting the point:

'"Except of me Mary my dear as your valentine and think over what I've said. – My dear Mary I will now conclude." That's all,' said Sam.

'That's rather a sudden pull up, ain't it, Sammy?' inquired Mr Weller.

'Not a bit on it,' said Sam; 'she'll wish there wos more, and that's the great art o' letter writin'.'

'Well,' said Mr Weller, 'there's somthin' in that; and I wish your mother-in-law 'ud only conduct her conversation on the same genteel principle. Ain't you a goin' to sign it?'

'That's the difficulty,' said Sam; 'I don't know what *to* sign it.'

'Sign it, Weller,' said the oldest surviving proprietor of that name.

'Won't do,' said Sam. 'Never sign a valentine with your own name.'

'Sign it "Pickwick," then,' said Mr Weller; 'it's a verry good name, and a easy one to spell.'

'The very thing,' said Sam. 'I *could* end with a verse; what do you think?'

'I don't like it, Sam,' rejoined Mr Weller. 'I never know'd a respectable coachman as wrote poetry, 'cept one, as made an affectin' copy o' verses the night afore he wos hung for a highway robbery; and *he* wos only a **Camberwell** man, so even that's no rule.'

But Sam was not to be dissuaded from the poetical idea that had occurred to him, so he signed the letter,

'Your love-sick
Pickwick.'

And having folded it, in a very intricate manner, squeezed a downhill direction in one corner: 'To Mary, Housemaid, at Mr Nupkins's Mayor's, Ipswich, Suffolk;' and put it into his pocket, **wafered**, and ready for the General Post.

The Pickwick Papers

Glossary

Camberwell: an area of South London
wafered: sealed

Mr Bumble shows his wife who's boss

In this extract, Dickens enjoys describing a man who thinks he is lord and master within his own home, and especially lord and master of his newly-married wife, finding out that she is more than a match for him. She is not only unwilling to accept his authority, but determined to make everyone else around see that she is in charge. Bumble's pompous attempts to play the dominant role are doomed to failure. The comedy of the scene comes from his belief that women are feeble and inferior, against all the evidence that she is quicker, sharper, stronger and bolder than him.

Mr Bumble sat in the workhouse parlour, with his eyes moodily fixed on the cheerless grate, whence, as it was summer time, no brighter gleam proceeded, than the reflection of certain sickly rays of the sun, which were sent back from its cold and shining surface. A paper fly-cage dangled from the ceiling, to which he occasionally raised his eyes in gloomy thought; and, as the heedless insects hovered round the gaudy network, Mr Bumble would heave a deep sigh, while a more gloomy shadow overspread his **countenance**. Mr Bumble was **meditating**; it might be that the insects brought to mind some painful passage in his own past life.

Mr Bumble had married Mrs Corney, and was master of the workhouse. Another **beadle** had come into power. On him the cocked hat, gold-laced coat, and staff, had all three descended.

'And tomorrow two months it was done!' said Mr Bumble, with a sigh. 'It seems a age.'

Mr Bumble might have meant that he had concentrated a whole existence of happiness into the short space of eight weeks; but the sigh – there was a vast deal of meaning in the sigh.

'I sold myself,' said Mr Bumble, pursuing the same train of reflection, 'for six teaspoons, a pair of sugar tongs, and a milk pot; with a small quantity of second-hand furniture, and twenty pound in money. I went very reasonable. Cheap, dirt cheap!'

'Cheap!' cried a shrill voice in Mr Bumble's ear: 'you would have been dear at any price; and dear enough I paid for you, Lord above knows that!'

Mr Bumble turned, and encountered the face of his interesting **consort**, who, imperfectly **comprehending** the few words she had overheard of his complaint, had hazarded the foregoing remark at a venture.

'Is that,' said Mr Bumble with sentimental sternness, 'is that the voice as called me a irresistible duck? Is that the creetur that was all meekness, mildness, and sensibility?'

'It is indeed, worse luck,' replied his helpmate; 'not much of sensibility though, or I should have had more sense than to make the sacrifice I did.'

Glossary

countenance: face, expression

meditating: thinking deeply

beadle: parish official, a little like a constable

consort: husband or wife, usually of a king or queen

comprehending: understanding

'The sacrifice, Mrs Bumble?' said the gentleman with great **asperity**.

'You may well repeat the word,' rejoined the lady; 'it ought to be never out of my mouth, gracious knows.'

'I am not aware that it ever is, ma'am,' retorted Mr Bumble. 'It's always coming out of your mouth, ma'am, but is always there. Mrs Bumble, ma'am.'

'Well,' cried the lady.

'Have the goodness to look at me,' said Mr Bumble, fixing his eyes upon her. ('If she stands such a eye as that,' said Mr Bumble to himself, 'she can stand anything. It is a eye I never knew to fail with **paupers**, and if it fails with her my power is gone.')

Whether an exceedingly small expansion of eye be sufficient to quell paupers, who, being lightly fed, are in no very high condition; or whether the late Mrs Corney was particularly proof against eagle glances; are matters of opinion. The matter of fact is, that the matron was in no way overpowered by Mr Bumble's scowl, but, on the contrary, treated it with great **disdain**, and even raised a laugh **thereat**, which sounded as though it were genuine.

On hearing this most unexpected sound, Mr Bumble looked, first incredulous, and afterwards amazed. He then relapsed into his former state; nor did he rouse himself until his attention was again awakened by the voice of his partner.

'Are you going to sit snoring there, all day?' inquired Mrs Bumble.

'I am going to sit here, as long as I think proper, ma'am,' rejoined Mr Bumble; 'and although I was *not* snoring, I shall snore, gape, sneeze, laugh, or cry, as the humour strikes me; such being my **prerogative**.'

'*Your* prerogative!' sneered Mrs Bumble, with **ineffable** contempt.

'I said the word, ma'am,' said Mr Bumble. 'The pre-rogative of a man is to command.'

'And what's the prerogative of a woman, in the name of Goodness?' cried the **relict** of Mr Corney deceased.

'To obey, ma'am,' thundered Mr Bumble. 'Your late unfortunate husband should have taught it you; and then, perhaps, he might have been alive now. I wish he was, poor man!'

Mrs Bumble, seeing at a glance that the decisive moment had now arrived, and that a blow struck for the mastership on one side or other must necessarily be final and conclusive, no sooner heard this allusion to the dead and gone, than she dropped into a chair, and with a loud scream that Mr Bumble was a hard-hearted brute, fell into a **paroxysm** of tears.

But, tears were not the things to find their way to Mr Bumble's soul; his heart was waterproof. Like wash-able **beaver** hats that improve with rain, his nerves were rendered stouter and more vigorous by showers of tears, which, being tokens of weakness, and so far **tacit** admissions of his own power, pleased and exalted

Glossary

asperity: roughness

paupers: people with no money

disdain: scorn, contempt

thereat: at that

prerogative: right or privilege

ineffable: indescribable

relict: survivor from the past (widow)

paroxysm: sudden uncontrollable fit (of pain, anger or laughter)

beaver: fur

tacit: implied rather than spoken (silent)

him. He eyed his good lady with looks of great satisfaction, and begged, in an encouraging manner, that she should cry her hardest: the exercise being strongly conducive to health.

'It opens the lungs, washes the countenance, exercises the eyes, and softens down the temper,' said Mr Bumble. 'So cry away.'

As he discharged himself of this pleasantry, Mr Bumble took his hat from a peg, and putting it on, rather **rakishly**, on one side, as a man might, who felt he had asserted his superiority in a becoming manner, thrust his hands into his pockets, and sauntered towards the door, with much ease and **waggishness** depicted in his whole appearance.

Now, Mrs Corney that was, had great experience in matrimonial tactics, having, previous to the **bestowal** of her hand on Mr Corney, been united to another worthy gentleman, also departed. She had tried the tears, because they were less troublesome than a manual assault; but, she was quite prepared to **make trial of the latter** mode, as Mr Bumble was not long in discovering.

The first proof he experienced of the fact, was conveyed in a hollow sound, immediately succeeded by the sudden flying off of his hat to the opposite end of the room. This preliminary proceeding laying bare his head, the expert lady, clasping him tightly round the throat with one hand, inflicted a shower of blows (dealt with singular vigour and **dexterity**) upon it with the other. This done, she created a little variety by scratching his face, and tearing his hair; and, having, by this time, inflicted as much punishment as she **deemed** necessary for the offence, she pushed him over a chair, which was luckily well situated for the purpose: and defied him to talk about his prerogative again, if he dared.

'Get up!' said Mrs Bumble, in a voice of command. 'And take yourself away from here, unless you want me to do something desperate.'

Mr Bumble rose with a very rueful countenance: wondering much what something desperate might be. Picking up his hat, he looked towards the door.

'Are you going?' demanded Mrs Bumble.

'Certainly, my dear, certainly,' rejoined Mr Bumble, making a quicker motion towards the door. 'I didn't intend to – I'm going, my dear! You are so very violent, that really I –'

At this instant, Mrs Bumble stepped hastily forward to replace the carpet, which had been kicked up in the scuffle. Mr Bumble immediately darted out of the room, without bestowing another thought on his unfinished sentence: leaving the late Mrs Corney in full possession of the field.

'I couldn't have believed it,' said Mr Bumble, as he crawled down the passage arranging his disordered dress. 'She didn't seem one of that sort at all. If the paupers knew of this, I should be a **parochial bye-word**.'

⌐ Glossary ─────────────────

rakishly: jauntily, putting on a confident pose

waggishness: joking or humorous behaviour

bestowal: giving, placing, 'the bestowal of her hand' refers to their marriage

make trial of the latter: try a manual assault, i.e., physically attack him

dexterity: skill

deemed: considered

parochial bye-word: common topic of gossip in the parish

Mr Bumble was fairly taken by surprise, and fairly beaten. He had a decided **propensity** for bullying: derived no inconsiderable pleasure from the exercise of petty cruelty; and, consequently, was (it is needless to say) a coward. This is by no means a disparagement to his character; for many official personages, who are held in high respect and admiration, are the victims of similar **infirmities**. The remark is made, indeed, rather in his favour than otherwise, and with a view of impressing the reader with a just sense of his qualifications for office.

But, the measure of his degradation was not yet full. After making a tour of the house, and thinking, for the first time, that the poor-laws really were too hard on people; and that men who ran away from their wives, leaving them chargeable to the parish, ought, in justice, to be visited with no punishment at all, but rather rewarded as **meritorious** individuals who had suffered much; Mr Bumble came to a room where some of the female paupers were usually employed in washing the parish linen: whence the sound of voices in conversation now proceeded.

'Hem!' said Mr Bumble, summoning up all his native dignity. 'These women at least shall continue to respect the prerogative. Hallo! hallo there! What do you mean by this noise, you **hussies**?'

With these words, Mr Bumble opened the door, and walked in with a very fierce and angry manner: which was at once exchanged for a most humiliated and cowering air, as his eyes unexpectedly rested on the form of his lady wife.

'My dear,' said Mr Bumble, 'I didn't know you were here.'

'Didn't know I was here!' repeated Mrs Bumble. 'What do *you* do here?'

'I thought they were talking rather too much to be doing their work properly, my dear,' replied Mr Bumble: glancing distractedly at a couple of old women at the wash-tub, who were comparing notes of admiration at the workhouse-master's humility.

'*You* thought they were talking too much?' said Mrs Bumble. 'What business is it of yours?'

'Why, my dear –' urged Mr Bumble submissively.

'What business is it of yours?' demanded Mrs Bumble, again.

'It's very true, you're matron here, my dear,' submitted Mr Bumble; 'but I thought you mightn't be in the way just then.'

'I'll tell you what, Mr Bumble,' returned his lady. 'We don't want any of your interference. You're a great deal too fond of poking your nose into things that don't concern you, making everybody in the house laugh, the moment your back is turned, and making yourself look like a fool every hour in the day. Be off; come!'

Mr Bumble, seeing with excruciating feelings the delight of the two old paupers, who were tittering together most rapturously, hesitated for an instant. Mrs Bumble, whose patience brooked no delay, caught up a bowl of soap-suds, and motioning him towards the door, ordered him instantly to depart, on pain of receiving the contents upon his portly person.

Glossary

propensity: inclination towards, liking for

infirmities: weaknesses

meritorious: worthy, deserving

hussies: badly-behaved or worthless females

What could Mr Bumble do? He looked dejectedly round, and slunk away; and, as he reached the door, the titterings of the paupers broke into a shrill chuckle of delight. He was degraded in their eyes; he had lost **caste** and station before the very paupers; he had fallen from all the height and pomp of beadleship, to the lowest depth of the most snubbed henpeckery.

'All in two months!' said Mr Bumble, filled with dismal thoughts. 'Two months! No more than two months ago, I was not only my own master, but everybody else's, so far as the parochial workhouse was concerned, and now! –'

It was too much. Mr Bumble boxed the ears of the boy who opened the gate for him (for he had reached the portal in his **reverie**); and walked, distractedly, into the street.

Oliver Twist

Glossary

caste: position, standing
reverie: daydream

5
Table manners

Any close observer knows that people have personal gestures and habits. These may be as much a part of the person as a nose or a voice. Some people have characteristic movements, others have characteristic speech habits. They may wave their hands, fiddle with their hair or give a little cough when they start to speak. Being nervous or annoyed produces more of these giveaway signs. Novelists can use these mannerisms to help readers to visualize a character.

Dickens usually uses gestures and mannerisms for comic purposes but he also uses them to give an insight into character. One kind of activity he found really useful for details of character was eating. Many scenes in his novels are set at the dining-table, either at home or at an inn. Eating is useful to him as a novelist because it can bring out greed, fussiness, embarrassment or preferences in taste. The dining-table situations that follow work in different ways: to comment on the display of wealth and social connections, to show childhood anxiety and adult playfulness, and to show unpleasant aspects of personality.

These table scenes allow Dickens to bring out basic aspects of human character – perhaps because eating is such a basic activity, which makes us similar to animals if we slurp and munch or crunch and tear!

David and the very obliging waiter

Young David Copperfield is sent away to school by his cruel stepfather, Mr Murdstone. On his journey, he stops at an inn, where he meets a waiter who takes advantage of his innocent trust. Dickens makes David seem very naïve and vulnerable, and painfully embarrassed by the comments of others, but he doesn't make the waiter seem an inhuman exploiter. Dickens could have made the waiter a hateful villain, but he balances the account to be touching and comical rather than cruel and melodramatic.

I was wondering what would ultimately become of me, when a lady looked out of a bow-window where some fowls and joints of meat were hanging up, and said:

'Is that the little gentleman from Blunderstone?'

'Yes, ma'am,' I said.

'What name?' inquired the lady.

'Copperfield, ma'am,' I said.

'That won't do,' returned the lady. 'Nobody's dinner is paid for here, in that name.'

'Is it Murdstone, ma'am?' I said.

'If you're Master Murdstone,' said the lady, 'why do you go and give another name, first?'

I explained to the lady how it was, who then rang a bell, and called out, 'William! show the coffee-room!' upon which a waiter came running out of a kitchen on the opposite side of the yard to show it, and seemed a good deal surprised when he was only to show it to me.

It was a large long room with some large maps in it. I doubt if I could have felt much stranger if the maps had been real foreign countries, and I cast away in the middle of them. I felt it was taking a liberty to sit down, with my cap in my hand, on the corner of the chair nearest the door; and when the waiter laid a cloth on purpose for me, and put a set of **castors** on it, I think I must have turned red all over with modesty.

He brought me some chops, and vegetables, and took the covers off in such a bouncing manner that I was afraid I must have given him some offence. But he greatly relieved my mind by putting a chair for me at the table, and saying, very affably, 'Now, six-foot! come on!'

I thanked him, and took my seat at the board; but found it extremely difficult to handle my knife and fork with anything like **dexterity**, or to avoid splashing myself with the gravy, while he was standing opposite, staring so hard, and making me blush in the most dreadful manner every time I caught his eye. After watching me into the second chop, he said:

'There's half a pint of ale for you. Will you have it now?'

I thanked him and said, 'Yes.' Upon which he poured it out of a jug into a large tumbler, and held it up against the light, and made it look beautiful.

'My eye!' he said. 'It seems a good deal, don't it?'

┌─ **Glossary** ─────────────────────────────

castors: containers with pierced tops for sprinkling salt, pepper or sugar on food

dexterity: skill, competence

'It does seem a good deal,' I answered with a smile. For it was quite delightful to me, to find him so pleasant. He was a twinkling-eyed, pimple-faced man, with his hair standing upright all over his head; and as he stood with one **arm a-kimbo**, holding up the glass to the light with the other hand, he looked quite friendly.

'There was a gentleman here, yesterday,' he said – 'a stout gentleman, by the name of Topsawyer – perhaps you know him?'

'No,' I said 'I don't think –'

'In breeches and gaiters, broad-brimmed hat, grey coat, speckled **choker**,' said the waiter.

'No,' I said bashfully, 'I haven't the pleasure –'

'He came in here,' said the waiter, looking at the light through the tumbler, 'ordered a glass of ale – *would* order it – I told him not – drank it, and fell dead. It was too old for him. It oughtn't to be drawn; that's the fact.'

I was very much shocked to hear of this melancholy accident, and said I thought I had better have some water.

'Why you see,' said the waiter, still looking at the light through the tumbler, with one of his eyes shut up, 'our people don't like things being ordered and left. It offends 'em. But *I*'ll drink it, if you like. I'm used to it, and use is everything. I don't think it'll hurt me, if I throw my head back, and take it off quick. Shall I?'

I replied that he would much oblige me by drinking it, if he thought he could do it safely, but by no means otherwise. When he did throw his head back, and take it off quick, I had a horrible fear, I confess, of seeing him meet the fate of the lamented Mr Topsawyer, and fall lifeless on the carpet. But it didn't hurt him. On the contrary, I thought he seemed the fresher for it.

'What have we got here?' he said, putting a fork into my dish. 'Not chops?'

'Chops,' I said.

'Lord bless my soul!' he exclaimed, 'I didn't know they were chops. Why, a chop's the very thing to take off the bad effects of that beer! Ain't it lucky?'

So he took a chop by the bone in one hand, and a potato in the other, and ate away with a very good appetite, to my extreme satisfaction. He afterwards took another chop, and another potato; and after that, another chop and another potato. When we had done, he brought me a pudding, and having it before me, seemed to **ruminate**, and to become absent in his mind for some moments.

'How's the pie?' he said rousing himself.

'It's a pudding,' I made answer.

'Pudding!' he exclaimed. 'Why, bless me, so it is! What!' looking at it nearer. 'You don't mean to say it's a batter-pudding!'

'Yes, it is indeed.'

'Why, a batter-pudding,' he said, taking up a table-spoon, 'is my favourite pudding! Ain't that lucky? Come on, little 'un, and let's see who'll get most.'

The waiter certainly got most. He **entreated** me more than once to come in and win, but what with his table-spoon to my tea-spoon, his dispatch to my dispatch, and his appetite to my appetite, I was left far

---

Glossary

arm a-kimbo: hand on hip, elbow sticking out
choker: large neckerchief worn high under the chin
ruminate: meditate or ponder
entreated: begged or pleaded

behind at the first mouthful, and had no chance with him. I never saw anyone enjoy a pudding so much, I think; and he laughed, when it was all gone, as if his enjoyment of it lasted still.

Finding him so very friendly and companionable, it was then that I asked for the pen and ink and paper, to write to Peggotty. He not only brought it immediately, but was good enough to look over me while I wrote the letter. When I had finished it, he asked me where I was going to school.

I said, 'Near London,' which was all I knew.

'Oh! my eye!' he said, looking very low-spirited, 'I am sorry for that.'

'Why?' I asked him.

'Oh, Lord!' he said, shaking his head, 'that's the school where they broke the boy's ribs – two ribs – a little boy he was. I should say he was – let me see – how old are you, about?'

I told him between eight and nine.

'That's just his age,' he said. 'He was eight years and six months old when they broke his first rib; eight years and eight months old when they broke his second, and did for him.'

I could not disguise from myself, or from the waiter, that this was an uncomfortable coincidence, and inquired how it was done. His answer was not cheering to my spirits, for it consisted of two dismal words, 'With whopping.'

The blowing of the coach-horn in the yard was a **seasonable** diversion, which made me get up and hesitatingly inquire, in the mingled pride and **diffidence** of having a purse (which I took out of my pocket), if there were anything to pay.

'There's a sheet of letter-paper,' he returned. 'Did you ever buy a sheet of letter-paper?'

I could not remember that I ever had.

'It's dear,' he said, 'on account of the duty. Threepence. That's the way we're taxed in this country. There's nothing else, except the waiter. Never mind the ink. *I* lose by that.'

'What should you – what should I – how much ought I to – what would it be right to pay the waiter, if you please?' I stammered, blushing.

'If I hadn't a family, and that family hadn't the cowpock,' said the waiter, 'I wouldn't take a sixpence. If I didn't support a aged pairint, and a lovely sister,' – here the waiter was greatly agitated – 'I wouldn't take a farthing. If I had a good place, and was treated well here, I should beg acceptance of a trifle, instead of taking of it. But I live on broken **wittles** – and I sleep on the coals' – here the waiter burst into tears.

I was very much concerned for his misfortunates, and felt that any recognition short of ninepence would be mere brutality and hardness of heart. Therefore I gave him one of my three bright shillings, which he received with much humility and veneration, and spun up with this thumb, directly afterwards, to try the goodness of.

It was a little disconcerting to me, to find, when I was being helped up behind the coach, that I was supposed to have eaten all the dinner without any assistance. I discovered this, from overhearing the lady in the bow-window say to the guard, 'Take care of that

Glossary

seasonable: timely, convenient
diffidence: shyness, uncertainty
wittles: food (victuals). Broken wittles are leftovers

child, George, or he'll burst!' and from observing that
the women-servants who were about the place came
out to look and giggle at me as a young phenomenon.
My unfortunate friend the waiter, who had quite recovered his spirits, did not appear to be disturbed by
this, but joined in the general admiration without being at all confused. If I had any doubt of him, I suppose
this half awakened it; but I am inclined to believe that
with the simple confidence of a child, and the natural
reliance of a child upon superior years (qualities I am
very sorry any children should prematurely change for
wordly wisdom), I had no serious mistrust of him on
the whole, even then.

I felt it rather hard, I must own, to be made, without
deserving it, the subject of jokes between the coachman and guard as to the coach drawing heavy behind,
on account of my sitting there, and as to the greater
expediency of my travelling by waggon. The story of
my supposed appetite getting wind among the outside
passengers, they were merry upon it likewise; and
asked me whether I was going to be paid for, at school,
as two brothers or three, and whether I was contracted
for, or went upon the regular terms; with other pleasant questions. But the worst of it was, that I knew I
should be ashamed to eat anything, when an opportunity offered, and that, after a rather light dinner, I
should remain hungry all night – for I had left
my cakes behind, at the hotel, in my hurry. My
apprehensions were realized. When we stopped for
supper I couldn't muster courage to take any, though
I should have liked it very much, but sat by the fire and
said I didn't want anything. This did not save me from
more jokes, either; for a husky-voiced gentleman with
a rough face, who had been eating out of a sandwich-
box nearly all the way, except when he had been

drinking out of a bottle, said I was like a boa constrictor who took enough at one meal to last him a long time; after which, he actually bought a rash out upon himself with boiled beef.

David Copperfield

Glossary

expediency: suitability, more advisable course of action
apprehensions: anxious expectations

The great bread-eating contest: Joe and Pip

Some adults in Dickens' novels are shown to be warm and understanding in their dealings with children. Joe, Pip's brother-in-law, is especially kind to him, perhaps because he's rather like a child himself. Here, he tries to get Pip to play a favourite dinner-time game – seeing who can chew off the biggest hunk of bread. This goes on behind Mrs Joe's back, as she would not approve of such a foolish activity. Pip does not want to join in because he wants to save the bread for the convict who threatened to tear his heart and liver out if he didn't fetch him some food. Pip doesn't want to disappoint Joe and he doesn't want to get on the wrong side of Mrs Joe, but he is terrified of failing to do what the convict ordered.

My sister had a **trenchant** way of cutting our bread-and-butter for us, that never varied. First, with her left hand, she jammed the loaf hard and fast against her bib – where it sometimes got a pin into it, and sometimes a needle, which we afterwards got into our mouths. Then, she took some butter (not too much) on a knife, and spread it on the loaf, in an **apothecary** kind of way, as if she were making a **plaister** – using both sides of the knife with a slapping **dexterity**, and trimming and moulding the butter off round the crust. Then, she gave the knife a final smart wipe on the edge of the plaister, and then sawed a very thick round off the loaf; which she finally, before separating from the loaf, hewed into two halves, of which Joe got one, and I got the other.

On the present occasion, though I was hungry, I dared not eat my slice. I felt I must have something in reserve for my dreadful acquaintance, and his ally the still more dreadful young man. I knew Mrs Joe's housekeeping to be of the strictest kind, and that my **larcenous researches** might find nothing available in the safe. Therefore I resolved to put my hunk of bread-and-butter down the leg of my trousers.

The effort of resolution necessary to the achievement of this purpose, I found to be quite awful. It was as if I had to make up my mind to leap from the top of a high house, or plunge into a great depth of water. And it was made the more difficult by the unconscious Joe. In our already-mentioned **freemasonry** as fellow sufferers, and in his good-natured companionship with me, it was our evening habit to compare the way we bit through our slices, by silently holding them up to each other's admiration now and then – which stimulated us to new exertions. Tonight, Joe several times invited me, by the display of his fast-diminishing slice, to enter upon our usual friendly competition; but he found me, each time, with my yellow mug of tea on one knee, and

Glossary

trenchant: forceful, vigorous

apothecary: medical practitioner, less qualified than a doctor, who made and sold medicines, usually from his own shop

plaister: sticky setting mixture (as in a plaster put on a broken limb)

dexterity: skill, competence

larcenous researches: looking to see what food he might be able to steal; 'larcenous' means 'thieving'

freemasonry: membership of a secret society

my untouched bread-and-butter on the other. At last, I desperately considered that the thing I contemplated must be done, and that it had best be done in the least improbable manner consistent with the circumstances. I took advantage of a moment when Joe had just looked at me, and got my bread-and-butter down my leg.

Joe was evidently made uncomfortable by what he supposed to be my loss of appetite, and took a thoughtful bite out of his slice, which he didn't seem to enjoy. He turned it about in his mouth much longer than usual, pondering over it a good deal, and after all gulped it down like a pill. He was about to take another bite, and had just got his head on one side for a good **purchase** on it, when his eye fell on me, and he saw that my bread-and-butter was gone.

The wonder and **consternation** with which Joe stopped on the threshold of his bite and stared at me were too evident to escape my sister's observation.

'What's the matter now?' said she smartly, as she put down her cup.

'I say, you know!' muttered Joe, shaking his head at me in very serious **remonstrance**. 'Pip old chap! You'll do yourself a mischief. It'll stick somewhere. You can't have chawed it, Pip.'

'What's the matter *now*?' repeated my sister, more sharply than before.

'If you can cough any trifle on it up, Pip, I'd recommend you to do it,' said Joe, all aghast. 'Manners is manners, but still your elth's your elth.'

By this time, my sister was quite desperate, so she pounced on Joe, and, taking him by the two whiskers, knocked his head for a little while against the wall behind him: while I sat in the corner, looking guiltily on.

'Now, perhaps you'll mention what's the matter,' said my sister, out of breath, 'you staring great stuck pig.'

Joe looked at her in a helpless way; then took a helpless bite, and looked at me again.

'You know, Pip,' said Joe solemnly, with his last bite in his cheek, and speaking in a confidential voice, as if we two were quite alone, 'you and me is always friends, and I'd be the last to tell upon you, any time. But such a' – he moved his chair and looked about the floor between us, and then again at me – 'such a most uncommon bolt as that!'

'Been bolting his food, has he?' cried my sister.

'You know, old chap,' said Joe, looking at me, and not at Mrs Joe, with his bite still in his cheek, 'I Bolted, myself, when I was your age – frequent – and as a boy I've been among a many Bolters; but I never see your Bolting equal yet, Pip, and it's a mercy you an't Bolted dead.'

My sister made a dive at me, and fished me up by the hair: saying nothing more than the awful words, 'You come along and be dosed.'

Some medical beast had revived Tar-water in those days as a fine medicine, and Mrs Joe always kept a supply of it in the cupboard; having a belief in its virtues correspondent to its nastiness. At the best of times, so much of this **elixir** was administered to me as

Glossary

purchase: leverage

consternation: anxious concern

remonstrance: reproach, protest

elixir: potion thought to prolong life or cure anything

a choice restorative, that I was conscious of going about, smelling like a new fence. On this particular evening, the urgency of my case demanded a pint of this mixture, which was poured down my throat, for my greater comfort, while Mrs Joe held my head under her arm, as a boot would be held in a boot-jack. Joe got off with half a pint; but was made to swallow that (much to his disturbance, as he sat slowly munching and meditating before the fire), 'because he had a turn.' Judging from myself, I should say he certainly had a turn afterwards, if he had had none before.

Great Expectations

Dinner with the Veneerings

This passage describes the social life of the recently-rich Veneerings. Since coming into money they have bought themselves all the fashionable luxuries that go with high-society status. The one thing they lack, though, is high-society friends. Dickens uses the passage to comment on a change in Victorian society, where people who made money out of industry were becoming wealthier than some who were born into the aristocracy. The Veneerings are delighted to find a poor aristocrat whom they can adopt and pretend they have known for years, showing him off to their friends at dinner parties. He doesn't have to do anything; he just has to be there – an ornamental part of their dining-room furniture.

M r and Mrs Veneering were bran-new people in a bran-new house in a bran-new quarter of London. Everything about the Veneerings was spick and span new. All their furniture was new, all their friends were new, all their servants were new, their plate was new, their carriage was new, their harness was new, their horses were new, their pictures were new, they themselves were new, they were as newly married as was lawfully compatible with their having a bran-new baby, and if they had set up a great-grandfather, he would have come home in matting from the

Pantechnicon, without a scratch upon him, French polished to the crown of his head.

For, in the Veneering establishment, from the hall chairs with the new coat of arms, to the grand pianoforte with the new action, and upstairs again to the new fire escape, all things were in a state of high varnish and polish. And what was observable in the furniture, was observable in the Veneerings – the surface smelt a little too much of the workshop and was a trifle stickey.

There was an innocent piece of dinner-furniture that went upon easy **castors** and was kept over a livery stable yard in Duke Street, Saint James's, when not in use, to whom the Veneerings were a source of blind confusion. The name of this article was Twemlow. Being first cousin to Lord Snigsworth, he was in frequent **requisition**, and might be said to represent the dining-table in its normal state. Mr and Mrs Veneering, for example, arranging a dinner, habitually started with Twemlow, and then put **leaves** in him, or added guests to him. Sometimes, the table consisted of Twemlow and half a dozen leaves; sometimes, of Twemlow and a dozen leaves; sometimes, Twemlow was pulled out to his utmost extent of twenty leaves. Mr and Mrs Veneering on occasions of ceremony faced each other in the centre of the board, and thus the parallel still held; for, it always happened that the more Twemlow was pulled out, the further he found himself from the centre, and the nearer to the sideboard at one end of the room, or the window-curtains at the other.

But, it was not this which steeped the feeble soul of Twemlow in confusion. This he was used to, and could take soundings of. The abyss to which he could find no bottom, and from which started forth the engrossing and ever-swelling difficulty of his life, was the insoluble question whether he was Veneering's oldest friend, or newest friend. To the **excogitation** of this problem, the harmless gentleman had devoted many anxious hours, both in his lodgings over the livery stable yard, and in the cold gloom, favourable to meditation, of Saint James's Square. Thus, Twemlow had first known Veneering at his club, where Veneering then knew nobody but the man who made them known to one another, who seemed to be the most intimate friend he had in the world, and whom he had known two days – the bond of union between their souls, the **nefarious** conduct of the committee respecting the cookery of a fillet of veal, having been accidently cemented at that date. Immediately upon this, Twemlow received an invitation to dine with the man, and dined: Veneering being of the party. At the man's were a Member, an Engineer, a Payer-off of the National Debt, a Poem on Shakespeare, a Grievance, and a Public Office, who all seemed to be utter strangers to Veneering. And yet immediately after that, Twemlow received an invitation to dine at Veneerings, expressly to meet the Member, the Engineer, the Payer-off of the National Debt, the Poem on Shakespeare, the Grievance, and the Public Office, and, dining, discovered

Glossary

pantechnicon: furniture warehouse

castors: little wheels

requisition: use

leaves: extra sections of the table

excogitation: working something out by deep thinking

nefarious: disgraceful, very wicked

that all of them were the most intimate friends Veneering had in the world, and that the wives of all of them (who were all there) were the objects of Mrs Veneering's most devoted affection and tender confidence.

Thus it had come about, that Mr Twemlow had said to himself in his lodgings, with his hand to his forehead: 'I must not think of this. This is enough to soften any man's brain,' – and yet was always thinking of it, and could never form a conclusion.

This evening the Veneerings give a banquet. Eleven leaves in the Twemlow; fourteen in company all told. Four pigeon-breasted retainers in plain clothes stand in line in the hall. A fifth retainer, proceeding up the staircase with a mournful air – as who should say, 'Here is another wretched creature come to dinner; such is life!' – announces, 'Mis-ter Twemlow!'

Our Mutual Friend

6
Home is where the English heart is

Dickens knew that we are most ourselves when we are at home. He liked to show how personality is reflected in space and belongings, how someone's private life may be different from the one shown to the world. In these extracts, Dickens shows how the word 'home' *can* mean security and happiness, but may also be less cosy and rosy than Victorians liked to believe.

Dickens also looked beyond the walls of a single dwelling to the country at large, to England as a nation. He saw in those who feel confidently 'at home' in England a national habit of thinking foreigners inferior. Not all English men and women share this foolish and arrogant attitude, but Dickens points out that a nation which has been cut off by water and language from its neighbours, may tend to think itself better than it is because it is does not know enough about its neighbours.

Foreigners: The view from Bleeding Heart Yard

Dickens often makes fun of the English habit of laughing at foreigners because they seem ignorant of our ways and our language. Here, he creates a comical picture of the way the Bleeding Heart Yard residents think they are helping the Italian to learn English. Dickens also describes the kind of stereotyped views that many English people had of people from other countries, all of them based on the assumption that 'British is Best'.

The foreigner, by name John Baptist Cavalletto – they called him Mr Baptist in the Yard – was a chirping, easy, hopeful little fellow. Solitary, weak, and **scantily acquainted** with the most necessary words of the only language in which he could communicate with the people about him, he went with the stream of his fortunes, in a brisk way that was new in those parts. With little to eat, and less to drink, and nothing to wear but what he wore upon him, or had brought tied up in one of the smallest bundles that ever were seen, he put as bright a face upon it as if he were in the most flourishing circumstances when he first hobbled up and down the Yard.

Glossary

scantily acquainted: barely familiar

Bleeding Heart Yard

It was uphill work for a foreigner, lame or sound, to make his way with the Bleeding Hearts. In the first place, they were persuaded that every foreigner had a knife about him; in the second, they held it to be a sound national **axiom** that he ought to go home to his own country. They never thought of inquiring how many of their own countrymen would be returned upon their hands from **divers** parts of the world, if the principle were generally recognized; they considered it particularly and peculiarly British. In the third place, they had a notion that it was a sort of Divine visitation upon a foreigner that he was not an Englishman, and that all kinds of calamities happened to his country because it did things that England did not, and did not do things that England did.

This, therefore, might be called a political position of the Bleeding Hearts; but they entertained other objections to having foreigners in the Yard. They believed that foreigners were always badly off; and though they were ill off themselves that did not diminish the force of the objection. They believed that foreigners were **dragooned and bayoneted**; and though they certainly got their own skulls promptly fractured if they showed any ill humour, still it was with a blunt instrument, and that didn't count. They believed that foreigners were always immoral; and though they had an occasional divorce case or so, that had nothing to do with it. They believed that foreigners had no independent spirit, as never being escorted to the poll in droves by **Lord Decimus Tite Barnacle**, with colours flying and the tune of Rule Britannia playing. Not to be tedious, they had many other beliefs of a similar kind.

Against these obstacles, the lame foreigner with the stick had to make head as well as he could. However, the Bleeding Hearts were kind hearts; and when they saw the little fellow cheerily limping about with a good-humoured face, doing no harm, drawing no knives, committing no outrageous immoralities, living chiefly on **farinaceous** and milk **diet**, and playing with children of an evening, they began to think that although he could never hope to be an Englishman, still it would be hard to **visit that affliction on his head**. They began to accommodate themselves to his level, calling him 'Mr Baptist,' but treating him like a baby, and laughing immoderately at his lively gestures and his childish English – more, because he didn't mind it, and laughed too. They spoke to him in very loud voices as if he were stone deaf. They constructed sentences, by way of teaching him the language in its purity, such as were addressed by the savages to Captain Cook, or by Friday to Robinson Crusoe. Mrs Plornish was particularly ingenious in this art; and **attained** so much celebrity for saying 'Me ope you leg well soon,' that it was considered in the Yard but a very short remove indeed from speaking Italian. Even Mrs Plornish her-

Glossary

axiom: well-established truth

divers: various

dragooned and bayoneted: bullied and ordered about by soldiers and stabbed with bayonets (a blade attached to a rifle barrel)

Lord Decimus Tite Barnacle: an imaginary parliamentary candidate

farinaceous diet: foods made from flour (such as spaghetti, macaroni, etc.)

visit that affliction on his head: to punish him further for being a foreigner

attained: achieved

self began to think that she had a natural call towards the language. As he became more popular, household objects were brought into **requisition** for his instruction in a **copious** vocabulary; and whenever he appeared in the Yard ladies would fly out at their doors crying 'Mr Baptist – tea-pot!' 'Mr Baptist – dust-pan!' 'Mr Baptist – flour-dredger!' 'Mr Baptist – **coffee-biggin**!' At the same time exhibiting those articles, and penetrating him with a sense of the appalling difficulties of the Anglo-Saxon tongue.

Little Dorritt

Glossary

requisition: use
copious: large, extensive
coffee-biggin: coffee pot with built-in strainer

The poorhouse

Oliver Twist is an orphan, brought up by the charity of the parish. He lives unhappily, in a foster-home run by Mrs Mann, who cares more for the money she gets than for the children she looks after. Now that he is nine, Oliver has to leave to live in the poorhouse. Dickens shows us how miserable it was to live in such a place, and how officials like Mr Bumble had no feeling for children, only love for the power and importance of their position.

Mrs Mann ushered the **beadle** into a small parlour with a brick floor; placed a seat for him, and **officiously** deposited his cocked hat and cane on the table before him.

'Now don't you be offended at what I'm a-going to say,' observed Mrs Mann, with captivating sweetness. 'You've had a long walk, you know, or I wouldn't mention it. Now, will you take a little drop of something, Mr Bumble?'

'Not a drop. Not a drop,' said Mr Bumble, waving his right hand in a dignified, but still placid manner.

'I think you will,' said Mrs Mann, who had noticed the tone of the refusal, and the gesture that had

---

Glossary

beadle: parish official, a little like a constable
officiously: dutifully

accompanied it. 'Just a *leetle* drop, with a little cold water, and a lump of sugar.'

Mr Bumble coughed.

'Now, just a little drop,' said Mrs Mann persuasively.

'What is it?' inquired the beadle.

'Why, it's what I'm obliged to keep a little of in the house, to put into the blessed infants' **Daffy**, when they ain't well, Mr Bumble,' replied Mrs Mann as she opened a corner cupboard, and took down a bottle and glass. 'It's gin. I'll not deceive you, Mr B.. It's gin.'

'Do you give the children Daffy, Mrs Mann?' inquired Bumble, following with his eyes the interesting process of mixing.

'Ah, bless 'em, that I do, dear as it is,' replied the nurse. 'I couldn't see 'em suffer before my very eyes, you know, sir.'

'No,' said Mr Bumble approvingly; 'no, you could not. You are a humane woman, Mrs Mann.' – (Here she set down the glass.) – 'I shall take an early opportunity of mentioning it to the board, Mrs Mann.' – (He drew it towards him.) – 'I – I drink your health with cheerfulness, Mrs Mann'; – and he swallowed half of it.

'And now about business,' said the beadle, taking out a leathern pocket-book. 'The child that was half-baptized Oliver Twist, is nine year old today.'

'Bless him!' interposed Mrs Mann, inflaming her left eye with the corner of her apron.

'And notwithstanding a reward of ten pound, which was afterwards increased to twenty pound, – notwithstanding the most supernat'ral exertions on the part of this parish,' said Bumble, 'we have never been able to discover who is his father, or what was his mother's name, or condition.'

Mrs Mann raised her hands in astonishment; but added, after a moment's reflection, 'How comes he to have any name at all, then?'

The beadle drew himself up with great pride, and said, 'I invented it.'

'You, Mr Bumble!'

'I, Mrs Mann. We name our **fondlings** in alphabetical order. The last was a S, – Swubble, I named him. This was a T, – Twist, I named *him*. The next one as comes will be Unwin, and the next Vilkins. I have got names ready made to the end of the alphabet, and all the way through it again, when we come to Z.'

'Why, you're quite a literary character, sir!' said Mrs Mann.

'Well, well,' said the beadle, gratified with the compliment; 'perhaps I may be, – perhaps I may be, Mrs Mann.' He finished the gin-and-water, and added, 'Oliver being now too old to remain here, the board have determined to have him back into the house, and I have come out myself to take him there, – so let me see him at once.'

'I'll fetch him directly,' said Mrs Mann, leaving the room for that purpose. And Oliver, having had by this time as much of the outer coat of dirt, which encrusted his face and hands, removed, as could be scrubbed off in one washing, was led into the room by his benevolent protectress.

'Make a bow to the gentleman, Oliver,' said Mrs Mann.

Glossary

Daffy: tonic or general medicine

fondlings: foundlings, i.e., orphans

Oliver made a bow, which was divided between the beadle on the chair and the cocked hat on the table.

'Will you go along with me, Oliver?' said Mr Bumble in a majestic voice.

Oliver was about to say that he would go along with anybody with great readiness, when, glancing upward, he caught sight of Mrs Mann, who had got behind the beadle's chair, and was shaking her fist at him with a furious countenance. He took the hint at once, for the fist had been too often impressed upon his body not to be deeply impressed upon his recollection.

'Will *she* go with me?' inquired poor Oliver.

'No, she can't,' replied Mr Bumble. 'But she'll come and see you sometimes.'

This was no very great consolation to the child; but, young as he was, he had sense enough to **make a feint of** feeling great regret at going away. It was no very difficult matter for the boy to call tears into his eyes. Hunger and ill-usage are great assistants if you want to cry; and Oliver cried very naturally indeed. Mrs Mann gave him a thousand embraces, and, what Oliver wanted a great deal more, a piece of bread and butter, lest he should seem too hungry when he got to the workhouse. With the slice of bread in his hand, and the little brown parish cap on his head, Oliver was then led away by Mr Bumble from the wretched home where one kind word or look had never lighted the gloom of his infant years. And yet he burst into an agony of childish grief as the cottage gate closed after him. Wretched as were the little companions in misery he was leaving behind, they were the only friends he had ever known; and a sense of his loneliness in the great wide world sank into the child's heart for the first time.

Mr Bumble walked on with long strides, and little Oliver, firmly grasping his gold-laced cuff, trotted beside him, inquiring at the end of every quarter of a mile whether they were 'nearly there'. To these interrogations Mr Bumble returned brief and snappish replies; for the temporary blandness which gin-and-water awakens in some bosoms had by this time evaporated, and he was once again a beadle.

Oliver had not been within the walls of the workhouse a quarter of an hour, and had scarcely completed a second slice of bread, when Mr Bumble, who had handed him over to the care of an old woman, returned, and, telling him it was a board night, informed him that the board had said he was to appear before it forthwith.

Not having a very clearly defined notion of what a board was, Oliver was rather astounded, and not quite certain whether he ought to laugh or cry. He had no time to think about the matter, however; for Mr Bumble gave him a tap on the head with his cane to wake him up, and another on the back to make him lively, and bidding him follow, conducted him into a large room where eight or ten fat gentlemen were sitting round a table, at the top of which, seated in an armchair rather higher than the rest, was a particularly fat gentleman with a very round, red face.

'Bow to the board,' said Bumble. Oliver brushed away two or three tears that were lingering in his eyes, and seeing no board but the table, bowed to that.

Glossary

make a feint of: make a pretence of

'What's your name, boy?' said the gentleman in the high chair.

Oliver was frightened at the sight of so many gentlemen, which made him tremble; and the beadle gave him another tap behind, which made him cry; and these two causes made him answer in a very low and hesitating voice; whereupon a gentleman in a white waistcoat said he was a fool. Which was a capital way of raising his spirits, and putting him quite at his ease.

'Boy,' said the gentleman in the high chair, 'listen to me. You know you're an orphan, I suppose?'

'What's that, sir?' inquired poor Oliver.

'The boy *is* a fool – I thought he was,' said the gentleman in the white waistcoat, in a very decided tone.

'Hush!' said the gentleman who had spoken first. 'You know you've got no father or mother, and that you were brought up by the parish, don't you?'

'Yes, sir,' replied Oliver, weeping bitterly.

'What are you crying for?' inquired the gentleman in the white waistcoat. And to be sure it was very extraordinary. What *could* the boy be crying for?

'I hope you say your prayers every night,' said another gentleman in a gruff voice, 'and pray for the people who feed you, and take care of you, like a Christian.'

'Yes, sir,' stammered the boy.

'Well! You have come here to be educated, and taught a useful trade,' said the red-faced gentleman in the high chair.

'So, you'll begin to **pick oakum** tomorrow morning at six o'clock,' added the surly one in the white waistcoat.

For the combination of both these blessings, Oliver bowed low by the direction of the beadle, and was then hurried away to a large ward, where, on a rough, hard bed, he sobbed himself to sleep. What a noble illustration of the tender laws of this favoured country! They let the paupers go to sleep!

***

The room in which the boys were fed was a large stone hall, with a copper at one end, out of which the master, dressed in an apron for the purpose, and assisted by one or two women, ladled the gruel at meal-times; of which each boy had one **porringer** and no more – except on festive occasions, and then he had two ounces and a quarter of bread besides. The bowls never wanted washing. The boys polished them with their spoons till they shone again; and when they had performed this operation (which never took very long, the spoons being nearly as large as the bowls), they would sit staring at the copper with such eager eyes as if they could have devoured the very bricks of which it was composed; employing themselves, meanwhile, in sucking their fingers most **assiduously**, with the view of catching up any stray splashes of gruel that might have been cast thereon. Boys have generally excellent appetites. Oliver Twist and his companions suffered the tortures of slow starvation for three months: at last they got so **voracious** and wild with hunger, that one boy, who was tall for his age, and hadn't been used

Glossary

pick oakum: pull old rope apart for recycling (a dirty, boring job given to convicts)

porringer: small bowl

assiduously: thoroughly

voracious: ravenous

Oliver asking for more

to that sort of thing, hinted darkly to his companions, that unless he had another basin of gruel *per diem*, he was afraid he might some night happen to eat the boy who slept next him, who happened to be a weakly youth of tender age. He had a wild, hungry eye; and they believed him. A council was held; lots were cast who should walk up to the master after supper that evening, and ask for more; and it fell to Oliver Twist.

The evening arrived; the boys took their places. The master, in his cook's uniform, stationed himself at the copper; his assistants ranged themselves behind him; the gruel was served out; and a long grace was said. The gruel disappeared; the boys whispered each other, and winked at Oliver, while his next neighbours nudged him. Child as he was, he was desperate with hunger, and reckless with misery. He rose from the table, and advancing to the master, basin and spoon in hand, said: somewhat alarmed at his own **temerity**:

'Please, sir, I want some more.'

The master was a fat, healthy man; but he turned very pale. He gazed in stupefied astonishment on the small rebel for some seconds, and then clung for support to the copper. The assistants were paralyzed with wonder; the boys with fear.

'What!' said the master at length, in a faint voice.

'Please, sir,' replied Oliver, 'I want some more.'

The master aimed a blow at Oliver's head with the ladle, pinioned him in his arms, and shrieked aloud for the beadle.

┌ Glossary

per diem: each day (Latin)
temerity: daring, recklessness

Oliver Twist

The board were sitting in solemn **conclave**, when Mr Bumble rushed into the room in great excitement, and addressing the gentleman in the high chair, said,

'Mr Limbkins, I beg your pardon, sir! Oliver Twist has asked for more!' There was a general start. Horror was depicted on every countenance.

'For *more*!' said Mr Limbkins. 'Compose yourself, Bumble, and answer me distinctly. Do I understand that he asked for more, after he had eaten the supper allotted by the dietary?'

'He did, sir,' replied Bumble.

'That boy will be hung,' said the gentleman in the white waistcoat; 'I know that boy will be hung.'

Nobody controverted the prophetic gentleman's opinion. An animated discussion took place. Oliver was ordered into instant confinement; and a bill was next morning pasted on the outside of the gate, offering a reward of five pounds to anybody who would take Oliver Twist off the hands of the parish. In other words, five pounds and Oliver Twist were offered to any man or woman who wanted an apprentice to any trade, business, or calling.

'I never was more convinced of anything in my life,' said the gentleman in the white waistcoat, as he knocked at the gate and read the bill next morning: 'I never was more convinced of anything in my life, than I am that that boy will come to be hung.'

Oliver Twist

Glossary

conclave: meeting

Christmas at the Cratchits'

Ebeneezer Scrooge is the tight-fisted, miserable employer of Bob Crachit. Scrooge hates Christmas, and hates the idea that people have time off work, and enjoy themselves. He realizes how wrong he is, and how much misery he has caused others, when one of the Spirits of Christmas visits him and takes him, invisibly, to see the lives of others. In this passage, Dickens makes the warmth and happiness of this poor family seem more precious than money and work.

It was the good Spirit's sympathy with all poor men that led him straight to Scrooge's clerk's; for there he went, and took Scrooge with him; and on the threshold of the door the Spirit smiled, and stopped to bless Bob Cratchit's dwelling. Think of that! Bob had but fifteen '**Bob**' a-week himself; he pocketed on Saturdays but fifteen copies of his Christian name; and yet the Ghost of Christmas Present blessed his four-roomed house!

Then up rose Mrs Cratchit, Cratchit's wife, dressed poorly in a twice-turned gown, but brave in ribbons, which are cheap and make a goodly show for sixpence; and she laid the cloth, assisted by Belinda Cratchit, second of her daughters, also brave in ribbons; while Master Peter Cratchit plunged a fork into the sauce-

Glossary

'**Bob**': in pre-decimal currency, a bob was a shilling (5p)

pan of potatoes, and getting the corners of his monstrous shirt collar (Bob's private property, conferred upon his son and heir in honour of the day) into his mouth, rejoiced to find himself so gallantly attired, and yearned to show his linen in the fashionable Parks. And now two smaller Cratchits, boy and girl, came tearing in, screaming that outside the baker's they had smelt the goose, and known it for their own; and basking in luxurious thoughts of sage and onion, these young Cratchits danced about the table and Master Peter Cratchit, while he (not proud, although his collars nearly choked him) blew the fire, until the slow potatoes bubbling up, knocked loudly at the saucepan lid to be let out and peeled.

'What has ever got your precious father then,' said Mrs Cratchit. 'And your brother, Tiny Tim; and Martha warn't as late last Christmas Day by half-an-hour!'

'Here's Martha, mother!' cried the two young Cratchits. 'Hurrah! There's *such* a goose, Martha!'

'Why, bless your heart alive, my dear, how late you are!' said Mrs Cratchit, kissing her a dozen times, and taking off her shawl and bonnet for her, with **officious** zeal.

'We'd a deal of work to finish up last night,' replied the girl, 'and had to clear away this morning, mother!'

'Well! Never mind so long as you are come,' said Mrs Cratchit. 'Sit ye down before the fire, my dear, and have a warm, Lord bless ye!'

'No no! There's father coming,' cried the two young Cratchits, who were everywhere at once. 'Hide Martha, hide!'

So Martha hid herself, and in came little Bob, the father, with at least three feet of **comforter** exclusive of the fringe, hanging down before him; and his threadbare clothes darned up and brushed; and Tiny Tim upon his shoulder. Alas for Tiny Tim, he bore a little crutch, and had his limbs supported by an iron frame!

'Why, where's our Martha?' cried Bob Cratchit looking round.

'Not coming,' said Mrs Cratchit.

'Not coming!' said Bob, with a sudden **declension** in his high spirits; for he had been Tim's horse all the way from church, 'Not coming upon Christmas Day!'

Martha didn't like to see him disappointed, if it were only in joke; so she came out from behind the closet door, and ran into his arms, while the two young Cratchits hustled Tiny Tim, and bore him off into the wash-house, that he might hear the pudding singing in the copper.

'And how did little Tim behave?' asked Mrs Cratchit, when Bob had hugged his daughter to his heart's content.

'As good as gold,' said Bob, 'and better. Somehow he gets thoughtful sitting by himself so much, and thinks the strangest things you ever heard. He told me, coming home, that he hoped the people saw him in the church, because he was a cripple, and it might be pleasant to them to remember upon Christmas Day, who made lame beggars walk and blind men see.'

Bob's voice was tremulous when he told them this, and trembled more when he said that Tiny Tim was growing strong and hearty.

Glossary

officious: dutiful, (here) motherly
comforter: woollen scarf
declension: fall

His active little crutch was heard upon the floor, and back came Tiny Tim, escorted by his brother and sister to his stool before the fire; and while Bob **compounded** some hot mixture in a jug with gin and lemons, and stirred it round and round and put it on the hob to simmer; Master Peter, and the two **ubiquitous** young Cratchits went to fetch the goose, with which they soon returned in high procession.

Such a bustle ensued that you might have thought a goose the rarest of all birds; a feathered phenomenon, to which a black swan was a matter of course; and in truth it was something very like it in that house. Mrs Cratchit made the gravy (ready beforehand in a little saucepan) hissing hot; Master Peter mashed the potatoes, Miss Belinda sweetened up the apple sauce; Martha dusted the hot plates; Bob took Tiny Tim beside him in a tiny corner at the table; the two young Cratchits set chairs for everybody, not forgetting themselves. At last the dishes were set on, succeeded by a breathless pause, as Mrs Cratchit, looking slowly all along the carving-knife, prepared to plunge it in the breast; but when she did, and when the long expected gush of stuffing issued forth, one murmur of delight arose all round the board, and even Tiny Tim, excited by the two young Cratchits, beat on the table with the handle of his knife, and feebly cried Hurrah!

There never was such a goose. Bob said he didn't believe there ever was such a goose cooked. Its tenderness and flavour, size and cheapness, were the themes of universal admiration. Eked out by the apple sauce and mashed potatoes, it was a sufficient dinner for the whole family. Every one had had enough, and the youngest Cratchits in particular, were steeped in sage and onion to the eyebrows! But now, the plates being changed by Miss Belinda, Mrs Cratchit left the room to take the pudding up, and bring it in.

Suppose it should not be done enough! Suppose it should break in turning out! Suppose somebody should have got over the wall of the backyard, and stolen it, while they were merry with the goose! All sorts of horrors were supposed. Hallo! A great deal of steam! The pudding was out of the copper. In half a minute Mrs Cratchit entered: flushed, but smiling proudly: with the pudding, like a speckled cannonball, so hard and firm, blazing in ignited brandy, and **bedight** with Christmas holly stuck into the top.

Oh, a wonderful pudding! Bob Cratchit said he regarded it as the greatest success achieved by Mrs Cratchit since their marriage. Mrs Cratchit said that now the weight was off her mind, she would confess she had had her doubts about the quantity of flour. Everybody had something to say about it, but nobody said or thought it was at all a small pudding for a large family. It would have been heresy to do so. Any Cratchit would have blushed to hint at such a thing.

At last the dinner was all done, the cloth was cleared, the hearth swept, and the fire made up. The compound in the jug being tasted, and considered perfect, apples and oranges were put upon the table, and a shovel-full of chestnuts on the fire. Then all the Cratchit family drew round the hearth, in what Bob Cratchit called a circle, meaning half a one; and at Bob Cratchit's elbow

Glossary

compounded: mixed together
ubiquitous: everywhere at once
bedight: decorated

stood the family display of glass; two tumblers, and a custard-cup without a handle.

These held the hot stuff from the jug, however, as well as golden goblets would have done; and Bob served it out with beaming looks, while the chestnuts on the fire sputtered and crackled noisily. Then Bob proposed:

'A Merry Christmas to us all, my dears. God bless us!'

Which all the family re-echoed.

'God bless us every one!' said Tiny Tim, the last of all.

Scrooge cast his eyes upon the ground. But he raised them speedily, on hearing his own name.

'Mr Scrooge!' said Bob; 'I'll give you Mr Scrooge, the Founder of the Feast!'

'The Founder of the Feast indeed!' cried Mrs Cratchit, reddening. 'I wish I had him here. I'd give him a piece of my mind to feast upon, and I hope he'd have a good appetite for it.'

'My dear,' said Bob, 'the children; Christmas Day.'

'It should be Christmas Day, I am sure,' said she, 'on which one drinks the health of such an odious, stingy, hard, unfeeling man as Mr Scrooge. You know he is, Robert! Nobody knows it better than you do, poor fellow!'

'My dear,' was Bob's mild answer, 'Christmas Day.'

'I'll drink his health for your sake and the Day's,' said Mrs Cratchit, 'not for his. Long life to him! A Merry Christmas and a Happy New Year! – he'll be very merry and very happy, I have no doubt!'

The children drank the toast after her. It was the first of their proceedings which had no heartiness in it. Tiny Tim drank it last of all, but he didn't care twopence for it. Scrooge was the Ogre of the family.

The mention of his name cast a dark shadow on the party, which was not dispelled for full five minutes.

After it had passed away, they were ten times merrier than before. Bob Cratchit told them how he had a situation in his eye for Master Peter, which would bring in, if obtained, full five-and-sixpence weekly. The two young Cratchits laughed tremendously at the idea of Peter's being a man of business; and Peter himself looked thoughtfully at the fire from between his collars, as if he were deliberating what particular investments he should favour when he came into that income. Martha, who was a poor apprentice at a milliner's, then told them what kind of work she had to do, and how many hours she worked at a stretch, and how she meant to lie a-bed tomorrow morning for a good long rest. All this time the chestnuts and the jug went round and round; and bye and bye they had a song, about a lost child travelling in the snow, from Tiny Tim; who had a plaintive little voice, and sang it very well indeed.

There was nothing of high mark in this. They were not a handsome family; they were not well dressed; their shoes were far from being waterproof; their clothes were scanty; and Peter might have known the inside of a pawnbroker's. But they were happy, grateful, pleased with one another, and contented with the time; and when they faded, and looked happier yet in the bright sprinklings of the Spirit's torch at parting, Scrooge had his eye upon them, and especially on Tiny Tim, until the last.

A Christmas Carol

7
Desperate situations

One of Dickens' successes as a writer was his ability to make people laugh. He did this not just for readers at home, but for audiences in theatres on his reading tours. As the readings in this country would sometimes bring in over £200 for a night's reading (a very great deal of money then) he was careful to write what the public would enjoy. But the popular taste was not only for comedy. Then, as now, readers enjoyed emotional tear-jerkers and dramatic cliff-hangers. His long novels were published in weekly or monthly episodes, so they were the equivalent of TV 'soap' serials today. Here are two extracts which show Dickens' ability to write entertainingly and movingly.

In *The Pickwick Papers* Mr Pickwick's mishaps – and his efforts to get out of them – ran for months as a serial, amusing readers with the adventures of a well-meaning but disaster-prone comic hero. In a very different vein, Dickens showed in *A Tale of Two Cities* how the Revolution in France spread fear, hatred and blind violence through the nation like a poison, destroying the good in people as it tried to get rid of the evil in society. He brought the great historical events home to readers as he made them experience the grisly and macabre last hours of life before execution. Dickens was able to use in fiction what he had seen in real life, not to entertain, but to make his readers think and feel about the wrongs of life – and to give them hope of something better.

Mr Pickwick and the wrong bedroom

Mr Pickwick is one of those people who, through no apparent fault of his own, gets into scrapes. Here, one thing leads to another until he finds himself in a potentially embarrassing and desperate situation, but he eventually manages to escape from it without disaster to himself or others.

'What's the time Mr Pickwick?'
'Past twelve.'

'Dear me, it's time to go to bed. It will never do, sitting here. I shall be pale tomorrow, Mr Pickwick.'

At the bare notion of such a **calamity**, Mr Peter Magnus rang the bell for the chambermaid; and the striped bag, the red bag, the leathern hatbox, and the brown-paper parcel, having been conveyed to his bedroom, he retired in company with a candlestick, to one side of the house, while Mr Pickwick, and another candlestick, were conducted through a multitude of tortuous windings, to another.

'This is your room, sir,' said the chambermaid.

'Very well,' replied Mr Pickwick, looking round him. It was a large double-bedded room, with a fire; upon the whole, a more comfortable-looking apartment than Mr Pickwick's short experience of the accommodations of the Great White Horse had led him to expect.

'Nobody sleeps in the other bed, of course,' said Mr Pickwick.

'Oh, no, sir.'

'Very good. Tell my servant to bring me up some hot water at half-past eight in the morning, and that I shall not want him any more tonight.'

'Yes, sir.' And bidding Mr Pickwick good night, the chambermaid retired, and left him alone.

Mr Pickwick sat himself down in a chair before the fire, and fell into a train of rambling meditations. First he thought of his friends, and wondered when they would join him; then his mind reverted to Mrs Martha Bardell; and from that lady it wandered to the dingy counting-house of Dodson and Fogg. From Dodson and Fogg's it flew off at a tangent, and then it came back to the Great White Horse at Ipswich, with sufficient clearness to convince Mr Pickwick that he was falling asleep. So he roused himself, and began to undress, when he recollected he had left his watch on the table down stairs.

Now, this watch was a special favourite with Mr Pickwick, having been carried about, beneath the shadow of his waistcoat, for a greater number of years than we feel called upon to state at present. The possibility of going to sleep, unless it were ticking gently beneath his pillow, had never entered Mr Pickwick's brain. So as it was pretty late now, and he was unwilling to ring his bell at that hour of the night, he slipped on his coat, of which he had just **divested** himself, and taking the candlestick in his hand, walked quietly down stairs.

The more stairs Mr Pickwick went down, the more stairs there seemed to be to descend, and again and

---

┌ Glossary

calamity: disaster
divested: taken off, removed

again, when Mr Pickwick got into some narrow passage, and began to congratulate himself on having gained the ground floor, did another flight of stairs appear before his astonished eyes. At last he reached a stone hall, which he remembered to have seen when he entered the house. Passage after passage did he explore; room after room did he peep into; at length, as he was on the point of giving up the search in despair, he opened the door of the identical room in which he had spent the evening, and beheld his missing property on the table.

Mr Pickwick seized the watch in triumph, and proceeded to retrace his steps to his bedchamber. If his progress downward had been attended with difficulties and uncertainty, his journey back was infinitely more perplexing. Rows of doors, garnished with boots of every shape, make, and size, branched off in every possible direction. A dozen times did he softly turn the handle of some bedroom door which resembled his own, when a gruff cry from within of 'Who the devil's that?' or 'What do you want here?' caused him to steal away, on tiptoe, with a perfectly marvellous **celerity**. He was reduced to the verge of despair, when an open door attracted his attention. He peeped in. Right at last! There were the two beds, whose situation he perfectly remembered, and the fire still burning. His candle, not a long one when he first received it, had flickered away in the drafts of air through which he had passed, and sank into the socket as he closed the door after him. 'No matter,' said Mr Pickwick, 'I can undress myself just as well by the light of the fire.'

The bedsteads stood one on each side of the door; and on the inner side of each was a little path, terminating in a rush-bottomed chair, just wide enough to admit of a person's getting into, or out of bed, on that side, if he or she thought proper. Having carefully drawn the curtains of his bed on the outside, Mr Pickwick sat down on the rush-bottomed chair, and leisurely divested himself of his shoes and **gaiters**. He then took off and folded up his coat, waistcoat, and neck-cloth, and slowly drawing on his tasselled nightcap, secured it firmly on his head, by tying beneath his chin the strings which he always had attached to that article of dress. It was at this moment that the absurdity of his recent bewilderment struck upon his mind. Throwing himself back in the rush-bottomed chair, Mr Pickwick laughed to himself so heartily, that it would have been quite delightful to any man of **well-constituted** mind to have watched the smiles that expanded his amiable features as they shone forth from beneath the nightcap.

'It is the best idea,' said Mr Pickwick to himself, smiling till he almost cracked the nightcap strings: 'It is the best idea, my losing myself in this place, and wandering about those staircases, that I ever heard of.' Here Mr Pickwick smiled again, a broader smile than before, and was about to continue the process of undressing, in the best possible humour, when he was suddenly stopped by a most unexpected interruption; to wit, the entrance into the room of some person with a candle, who, after locking the door, advanced to the dressing table, and set down the light upon it.

The smile that played on Mr Pickwick's features was instantaneously lost in a look of the most unbounded

---

┌─ **Glossary** ─────────────────────────

celerity: speed
gaiters: buttoned cloth coverings for the lower legs
well-constituted: well-formed, well-balanced

and wonder-stricken surprise. The person, whoever it was, had come in so suddenly and with so little noise, that Mr Pickwick had had no time to call out, or oppose their entrance. Who could it be? A robber? Some evil-minded person who had seen him come up stairs with a handsome watch in his hand, perhaps. What was he to do!

The only way in which Mr Pickwick could catch a glimpse of his mysterious visitor with the least danger of being seen himself, was by creeping on to the bed, and peeping out from between the curtains on the opposite side. To this manœuvre he accordingly resorted. Keeping the curtains carefully closed with his hand, so that nothing more of him could be seen than his face and nightcap, and putting on his spectacles, he mustered up courage, and looked out.

Mr Pickwick almost fainted with horror and dismay. Standing before the dressing-glass was a middle-aged lady, in yellow curl-papers, busily engaged in brushing what ladies call their 'back-hair.' However the unconscious middle-aged lady came into that room, it was quite clear that she contemplated remaining there for the night; for she had brought a rushlight and shade with her, which, with praiseworthy precaution against fire, she had stationed in a basin on the floor, where it was glimmering away, like a gigantic lighthouse in a particularly small piece of water.

'Bless my soul,' thought Mr Pickwick, 'what a dreadful thing!'

'Hem!' said the lady; and in went Mr Pickwick's head with automaton-like rapidity.

'I never met with anything so awful as this,' thought poor Mr Pickwick, the cold perspiration starting in drops under his nightcap. 'Never. This is fearful.'

Standing before the dressing-glass was a middle-aged lady ...

It was quite impossible to resist the urgent desire to see what was going forward. So out went Mr Pickwick's head again. The prospect was worse than before. The middle-aged lady had finished arranging her hair; had carefully enveloped it in a muslin nightcap with a small plaited border; and was gazing **pensively** on the fire.

'This matter is growing alarming,' reasoned Mr Pickwick with himself. 'I can't allow things to go in this way. By the self-possession of that lady it is clear to me that I must have come into the wrong room. If I call out she'll alarm the house; but if I remain here the consequences will be still more frightful.'

Mr Pickwick, it is quite unnecessary to say, was one of the most modest and delicate-minded of mortals. The very idea of exhibiting his nightcap to a lady overpowered him, but he had tied those confounded strings in a knot, and, do what he would, he couldn't get it off. The disclosure must be made. There was only one other way of doing it. He shrunk behind the curtains, and called out very loudly:

'Ha – hum!'

That the lady started at this unexpected sound was evident, by her falling up against the rushlight shade; that she persuaded herself it must have been the effect of imagination was equally clear, for when Mr Pickwick, under the impression that she had fainted away stone-dead from fright, ventured to peep out again, she was gazing pensively on the fire as before.

'Most extraordinary female this,' thought Mr Pickwick, popping in again. 'Ha – hum!'

These last sounds were too distinctly audible to be again mistaken for the workings of fancy.

'Gracious Heaven!' said the middle-aged lady, 'what's that?'

'It's – it's – only a gentleman, Ma'am,' said Mr Pickwick from behind the curtains.

'A gentleman!' said the lady with a terrific scream.

'It's all over!' thought Mr Pickwick.

'A strange man!' shrieked the lady. Another instant and the house would be alarmed. Her garments rustled as she rushed towards the door.

'Ma'am,' said Mr Pickwick, thrusting out his head, in the extremity of his desperation, 'Ma'am!'

Now, although Mr Pickwick was not actuated by any definite object in putting out his head, it was instantaneously productive of a good effect. The lady, as we have already stated, was near the door. She must pass it, to reach the staircase, and she would most undoubtedly have done so by this time, had not the sudden apparition of Mr Pickwick's nightcap driven her back into the remotest corner of the apartment, where she stood staring wildly at Mr Pickwick, while Mr Pickwick in his turn stared wildly at her.

'Wretch,' said the lady, covering her eyes with her hands, 'what do you want here?'

'Nothing, Ma'am; nothing, whatever, Ma'am;' said Mr Pickwick earnestly.

'Nothing!' said the lady, looking up.

'Nothing, Ma'am, upon my honour,' said Mr Pickwick, nodding his head so energetically that the tassel of his nightcap danced again. 'I am almost ready to sink, Ma'am, beneath the confusion of addressing a lady in my nightcap (here the lady hastily snatched off hers), but I can't get it off, Ma'am (here Mr Pickwick gave it a tremendous tug, in proof of the statement). It

Glossary

pensively: thoughtfully

is evident to me, Ma'am, now, that I have mistaken this bedroom for my own. I had not been here five minutes, Ma'am, when you suddenly entered it.'

'If this improbable story be really true, sir,' said the lady, sobbing violently, 'you will leave it instantly.'

'I will, Ma'am, with the greatest pleasure,' replied Mr Pickwick.

'Instantly, sir,' said the lady.

'Certainly, Ma'am,' interposed Mr Pickwick very quickly. 'Certainly, Ma'am. I – I – am very sorry, Ma'am,' said Mr Pickwick, making his appearance at the bottom of the bed, 'to have been the innocent occasion of this alarm and emotion; deeply sorry, Ma'am.'

The lady pointed to the door. One excellent quality of Mr Pickwick's character was beautifully displayed at this moment, under the most trying circumstances. Although he had hastily put on his hat over his nightcap, although he carried his shoes and gaiters in his hand, and his coat and waistcoat over his arm; nothing could subdue his native politeness.

'I am exceedingly sorry, Ma'am,' said Mr Pickwick, bowing very low.

'If you are, sir, you will at once leave the room,' said the lady.

'Immediately, Ma'am; this instant, Ma'am,' said Mr Pickwick, opening the door, and dropping both his shoes with a crash in so doing.

'I trust, Ma'am,' resumed Mr Pickwick, gathering up his shoes, and turning round to bow again: 'I trust, Ma'am, that my unblemished character, and the devoted respect I entertain for your sex, will plead as some slight excuse for this' – But before Mr Pickwick could conclude the sentence the lady had thrust him into the passage, and locked and bolted the door behind him.

Whatever grounds of self-congratulation Mr Pickwick might have for having escaped so quietly from his late awkward situation, his present position was by no means enviable. He was alone, in an open passage, in a strange house, in the middle of the night, half dressed; it was not to be supposed that he could find his way in perfect darkness to a room which he had been wholly unable to discover with a light, and if he made the slightest noise in his fruitless attempts to do so, he stood every chance of being shot at, and perhaps killed, by some wakeful traveller. He had no resource but to remain where he was until daylight appeared. So after groping his way a few paces down the passage, and, to his infinite alarm, stumbling over several pairs of boots in so doing, Mr Pickwick crouched into a little recess in the wall, to wait for morning as philosophically as he might.

The Pickwick Papers

Changing places in the shadow of the guillotine

Sydney Carton decides that he will give his own life for the sake of Lucie, the woman he loves. Lucie has married Charles Darnay, an aristocrat known as Evrémonde who has been condemned to death by the French Revolutionaries. Sydney has planned what he is to do in every detail, from using chloroform to drug Evrémonde to getting him to write down in a letter Sydney's own last words to Lucie.

C harles Darnay [also known as Evrémonde], alone in a cell, had sustained himself with no **flattering delusion** since he came to it from the Tribunal. In every line of the narrative he had heard, he had heard his **condemnation**. He had fully **comprehended** that no personal **influence** could possibly save him.

Nevertheless, it was not easy, with the face of his beloved wife fresh before him, to compose his mind to what it must bear. Before it had set in dark on the night of his condemnation, he sat down to write until such time as the prison lamps should be extinguished.

He wrote a long letter to Lucie. He besought her to devote herself to their dear child, as they would meet in heaven.

To her father he wrote that he expressly confided his wife and child to his care.

To **Mr Lorry** he explained his worldly affairs. That done, with many added sentences of grateful friendship and warm attachment, all was done. He never thought of Carton. His mind was so full of the others, that he never once thought of him.

He had never seen the instrument that was to terminate his life. How high it was from the ground, how many steps it had, where he would be stood, how he would be touched, whether the touching hands would be dyed red, which way his face would be turned, whether he would be the first, or might be the last: these and many similar questions **obtruded themselves** over and over again. Neither were they connected with fear: he was conscious of no fear. Rather, they originated in a strange desire to know what to do when the time came; a desire gigantically disproportionate to the few swift moments to which it referred.

The hours went on as he walked to and fro, and the clocks struck the numbers he would never hear again. Nine gone for ever, ten gone for ever, eleven gone for ever, twelve coming on to pass away. He walked up and down, softly repeating their names to himself. The worst of the strife was over. He could walk up and down, free from distracting **fancies**, praying for himself and for them.

Twelve gone for ever.

┌ Glossary

flattering delusion: false hope

condemnation: judgement, sentence (to death)

comprehended: understood

influence: power used on his behalf

Mr Lorry: a family friend and lawyer

obtruded themselves: came into his mind

fancies: imaginings

He had been **apprised** that the final hour was Three, and he knew he would be summoned some time earlier, inasmuch as the **tumbrils** jolted heavily and slowly through the streets. Therefore, he resolved to keep Two before his mind, as the hour, and so to strengthen himself in the interval that he might be able, after that time, to strengthen others.

Walking regularly to and fro with his arms folded on his breast, he heard One struck away from him, without surprise. The hour had measured like most other hours. Devoutly thankful to Heaven for his recovered self-possession, he thought, 'There is but another now,' and turned to walk again.

Footsteps in the stone passage outside the door. He stopped.

The key was put in the lock, and turned. Before the door was opened, or as it opened, a man said in a low voice, in English: 'He has never seen me here; I have kept out of his way. Go you in alone; I wait near. Lose no time!'

The door was quickly opened and closed, and there stood before him face to face, quiet, intent upon him, with the light of a smile on his features, and a cautionary finger on his lip, Sydney Carton.

There was something so bright and remarkable in his look, that, for the first moment, the prisoner misdoubted him to be an **apparition** of his own imagining. But, he spoke, and it was his voice; he took the prisoner's hand, and it was his real grasp.

'Of all the people upon earth, you least expected to see me?' he said.

'I could not believe it to be you. I can scarcely believe it now. You are not' – the apprehension came suddenly into his mind – 'a prisoner?'

'No. I am accidentally possessed of a power over one of the keepers here, and in virtue of it I stand before you. I come from her – your wife, dear Darnay.'

The prisoner wrung his hand.

'I bring you a request from her.'

'What is it?'

'A most earnest, pressing, and emphatic entreaty, addressed to you in the most pathetic tones of the voice so dear to you, that you well remember.'

The prisoner turned his face partly aside.

'You have no time to ask me why I bring it, or what it means; I have no time to tell you. You must comply with it – take off those boots you wear, and draw on these of mine.'

There was a chair against the wall of the cell, behind the prisoner. Carton, pressing forward, had already, with the speed of lightning, got him down into it, and stood over him, barefoot.

'Draw on these boots of mine. Quick!'

'Carton, there is no escaping from this place; it never can be done. You will only die with me. It is madness.'

'It would be madness if I asked you to escape; but do I? When I ask you to pass out at that door, tell me it is madness and remain here. Change that cravat for this of mine, that coat for this of mine. While you do it, let me take this ribbon from your hair, and shake out your hair like this of mine!'

┌ Glossary

apprised: informed
tumbrils: carts
apparition: phantom, imaginary form

With wonderful quickness, and a strength of will and action, he forced all these changes upon him. The prisoner was like a young child in his hands.

'Carton! Dear Carton! It is madness. It cannot be done, it has been attempted, and has always failed. I implore you not to add your death to the bitterness of mine.'

'Do I ask you, my dear Darnay, to pass the door? When I ask that, refuse. There are pen and ink and paper on this table. Is your hand steady enough to write?'

'It was when you came in.'

'Steady it again, and write what I shall dictate. Quick, friend, quick!'

Pressing his hand to his bewildered head, Darnay sat down at the table, Carton, with his right hand in his breast, stood close beside him.

'Write exactly as I speak.'

'To whom do I address it?'

'To no one.' Carton still had his hand in his breast.

'Do I date it?'

'No.'

The prisoner looked up, at each question. Carton, standing over him with his hand in his breast, looked down.

'"If you remember,"' said Carton, dictating '"the words that passed between us, long ago, you will readily comprehend this when you see it. You do remember them, I know. It is not in your nature to forget them."'

He was drawing his hand from his breast; the prisoner chancing to look up in his hurried wonder as he wrote, the hand stopped, closing upon something.

'Have you written "forget them"?' Carton asked.

'I have. Is that a weapon in your hand?'

'No; I am not armed.'

'What is it in your hand?'

'You shall know directly. Write on; there are but a few words more.' He dictated again. '"I am thankful that the time has come, when I can prove them. That I do so is no subject for regret or grief."' As he said these words with his eyes fixed on the writer, his hand slowly and softly moved down close to the writer's face.

The pen dropped from Darnay's fingers on the table, and he looked about him vacantly.

'What vapour is that?' he asked.

'Vapour?'

'Something that crossed me?'

'I am conscious of nothing; there can be nothing here. Take up the pen and finish. Hurry, hurry!'

As if his memory were impaired, or his **faculties** disordered, the prisoner made an effort to rally his attention. As he looked at Carton with clouded eyes and with an altered manner of breathing, Carton – his hand again in his breast – looked steadily at him.

'Hurry, hurry!'

The prisoner bent over the paper, once more.

'"If it had been otherwise;"' Carton's hand was again watchfully and softly stealing down; '"I never should have used the longer opportunity. If it had been otherwise;"' the hand was at the prisoner's face; "I should but have had so much the more to answer for. If it had been otherwise –"' Carton looked at the pen and saw it was trailing off into unintelligible signs.

Carton's hand moved back to his breast no more. The prisoner sprang up, but Carton's hand was close

┌ Glossary ───────────────────────────

faculties: wits, senses

and firm at his nostrils, and Carton's left arm caught him round the waist. For a few seconds he faintly struggled with the man who had come to lay down his life for him; but, within a minute or so, he was stretched **insensible** on the ground.

Quickly, but with hands as true to the purpose as his heart was, Carton dressed himself in the clothes the prisoner had laid aside, combed back his hair, and tied it with the ribbon the prisoner had worn. Then, he softly called, 'Énter there! Come in!' and **the Spy** presented himself.

'You see?' said Carton, looking up, as he kneeled on one knee beside the insensible figure, putting the paper in the breast: 'Now, get assistance and take me to the coach.'

'You?' said the Spy nervously.

'Him, man, with whom I have exchanged. You go out at the gate by which you brought me in?'

'Of course.'

'I was weak and faint when you brought me in, and I am fainter now you take me out. The parting interview has overpowered me. Such a thing has happened here, often, and too often. Quick! Call assistance! Take him yourself to the courtyard you know of, place him yourself in the carriage, show him yourself to Mr Lorry, tell him yourself to give him no restorative but air, and to remember my words of last night, and his promise of last night, and drive away!'

The Spy withdrew, and Carton seated himself at the table, resting his forehead on his hands. The Spy returned immediately, with two men.

'How, then?' said one of them, contemplating the fallen figure. 'So **afflicted** to find that his friend has drawn a prize in the lottery of Sainte Guillotine?'

They raised the unconscious figure, placed it on a **litter** they had brought to the door, and bent to carry it away.

'The time is short, Evrémonde,' said the Spy, in a warning voice.

'I know it well,' answered Carton. 'Be careful of my friend, I entreat you, and leave me.'

The door closed, and Carton was left alone. Straining his powers of listening to the utmost, he listened for any sound that might denote suspicion or alarm. There was none. Keys turned, doors clashed, footsteps passed along distant passages: no cry was raised, or hurry made, that seemed unusual. Breathing more freely in a little while, he sat down at the table, and listened again until the clock struck Two.

Sounds that he was not afraid of, for he **divined** their meaning, then began to be audible. Several doors were opened in succession and finally his own. A gaoler, with a list in his hand, looked in, merely saying, 'Follow me, Evrémonde!' and he followed into a large dark room. It was a dark winter day, and what with the shadows within, and what with the shadows without, he could but dimly **discern** the others who were brought there to have their arms bound. Some were

---

Glossary

insensible: unconscious
the Spy: a double agent
afflicted: moved, upset
litter: kind of stretcher
divined: guessed, understood
discern: see, make out

standing; some seated. Some were **lamenting**, and in restless motion; but, these were few. The great majority were silent and still, looking fixedly at the ground.

As he stood by the wall in a dim corner, while some of the fifty-two were brought in after him, one man stopped to embrace him, as having a knowledge of him. It thrilled him with a great dread of discovery; but the man went on. A very few moments after that, a young woman, with a slight girlish form, a spare face in which there was no **vestige** of colour, and large widely opened eyes, rose from where he had observed her sitting, and came to speak to him.

'Citizen Evrémonde,' she said, touching him with her cold hand. 'I am a poor little seamstress, who was with you in **La Force**.'

He murmured for answer: 'True. I forget what you were accused of?'

'Plots. Though Heaven knows I am innocent of any. Is it likely? Who would think of plotting with a poor little weak creature like me?'

'I am not afraid to die, Citizen Evrémonde, but I have done nothing. I am not unwilling to die, if the Republic which is to do so much good to us poor, will profit by my death; but I do not know how that can be, Citizen Evrémonde. Such a poor weak little creature! If I may ride with you, Citizen Evrémonde, will you let me hold your hand? I am not afraid, but I am weak, and it will give me more courage.'

As the patient eyes were lifted to his face, he saw a sudden doubt in them, and then astonishment. He pressed the work-worn, hunger-worn young fingers, and touched his lips.

'Are you dying for him?' she whispered.

'And his wife and child. Hush! Yes.'

'O you will let me hold your brave hand, stranger?'

'Hush! Yes, my poor sister; to the last.'

The footsteps die out for ever

Along the Paris streets, the death-carts rumble, hollow and harsh. Six tumbrils carry the day's wine to La Guillotine. All the devouring and **insatiate** Monsters imagined since imagination could record itself, are fused in the one realization, Guillotine. And yet there is not in France, with its rich variety of soil and climate, a blade, a leaf, a root, a sprig, a peppercorn, which will grow to maturity under conditions more certain than those that have produced this horror. Crush humanity out of shape once more, under similar hammers, and it will twist itself into the same tortured forms. Sow the same seed of licence and oppression again, and it will surely yield the same fruit.

Six tumbrils roll along the streets. As the sombre wheels of the six carts go round, they seem to plough up a long crooked furrow among the populace in the streets. Ridges of faces are thrown to this side and to that, and the ploughs go steadily onward. So used are the regular inhabitants of the houses to the spectacle, that in many windows there are no people, and in some the occupation of the hands is not so much as suspended, while the eyes survey the faces in the tumbrils. Here and there, the inmate has visitors to see the sight; then he points his finger, with something of the

Glossary

lamenting: crying, wailing
vestige: trace
La Force: a prison
insatiate: which cannot be satisfied

complacency of a curator or authorized exponent, to this cart and to this, and seems to tell who sat here yesterday, and who there the day before.

Of the riders in the tumbrils, some observe all things on their last roadside, with an impassive stare; others, with a lingering interest in the ways of life and men. Some, seated with drooping heads, are sunk in silent despair; again, there are some so heedful of their looks that they cast upon the multitude such glances as they have seen in theatres, and in pictures. Several close their eyes, and think or try to get their straying thoughts together. Only one, and he a miserable creature, of a crazed aspect, is so shattered and made drunk by horror, that he sings, and tries to dance. Not one of the whole number appeals by look or gesture, to the pity of the people.

There is a guard of horsemen riding abreast of the tumbrils, and faces are often turned up to some of them, and they are asked some question. It would seem to be always the same question, for, it is always followed by a press of people towards the third cart. The horsemen abreast of that cart, frequently point out one man in it with their swords. The leading curiosity is, to know which is he; he stands at the back of the tumbril with his head bent down, to converse with a mere girl who sits on the side of the cart, and holds his hand. He has no curiosity or care for the scene about him, and always speaks to the girl. Here and there in the long street, cries are raised against him. If they move him at all, it is only to a quiet smile, as he shakes his hair a little more loosely about his face. He cannot easily touch his face, his arms being bound.

The clocks are on the stroke of three, and the furrow ploughed among the populace is turning round, to come on into the place of execution, and end. The ridges thrown to this side and to that, now crumble in and close behind the last plough as it passes on, for all are following to the Guillotine. In front of it, seated in chairs, as in a garden of public **diversion**, are a number of women, busily knitting.

The tumbrils begin to discharge their loads. The ministers of Sainte Guillotine are robed and ready. Crash! – A head is held up, and the knitting-women who scarcely lifted their eyes to look at it a moment ago when it could think and speak, count One.

The second tumbril empties and moves on; the third comes up. Crash! – And the knitting-women, never faltering or pausing in their work, count Two.

The supposed Evrémonde descends, and the seamstress is lifted out next after him. He has not relinquished her hand in getting out, but still holds it as he promised. He gently places her with her back to the crashing engine that constantly whirrs up and falls, and she looks into his face and thanks him.

'But for you, dear stranger, I should not be so composed, for I am faint of heart. I think you were sent to me by Heaven.'

'Or you to me,' says Sydney Carton. 'Keep your eyes upon me, and mind no other object.'

'I mind nothing while I hold your hand. I shall mind nothing when I let it go, if they are rapid.'

'They will be rapid. Fear not!'

The two stand in the fast-thinning throng of victims, but they speak as if they were alone.

Glossary

diversion: entertainment

'Brave and generous friend, will you let me ask you one last question? I am very ignorant, and it troubles me – just a little.'

'Tell me what it is.'

'I have a cousin, whom I love very dearly. She is five years younger than I, and she lives in a farmer's house in the south, and she knows nothing of my fate – for I cannot write – and if I could, how should I tell her! It is better as it is.'

'Yes, yes; better as it is.'

'What I have been thinking as we came along, and what I am still thinking now, is this: – If the Republic really does good to the poor, and they come to be less hungry, and in all ways to suffer less, she may live a long time: she may even live to be old.'

'What then, my gentle sister?'

'Do you think:' the eyes fill with tears, and the lips part a little more and tremble: 'that it will seem long to me, while I wait for her in the better land where you and I will be mercifully sheltered?'

'It cannot be, my child; there is no Time there, and no trouble there.'

'You comfort me so much! I am so ignorant. Am I to kiss you now? Is the moment come?'

'Yes.'

She kisses his lips; he kisses hers; they solemnly bless each other. The spare hand does not tremble as he releases it. She goes next before him – is gone; the knitting-women count Twenty-Two.

'I am the Resurrection and the Life, saith the Lord: he that believeth in me, though he were dead, yet shall he live: and whosoever liveth and believeth in me shall never die.'

The murmuring of many voices, the upturning of many faces, the pressing on of many footsteps in the outskirts of the crowd, so that it swells forward in a mass, like one great heave of water, all flashes away. Twenty-Three.

***

They said of him, about the city that night, that it was the peacefullest man's face ever beheld there. Many added that he looked sublime and prophetic. If he had given an utterance to his thoughts, they would have been these: 'I see a beautiful city and a brilliant people rising from this abyss, and, in their struggles to be truly free, I see the evil of this time and of the previous time of which this is the natural birth, wearing out.

'I see the lives for which I lay down my life, peaceful, useful, prosperous and happy, in that England which I shall see no more. I see Her with a child upon her bosom, who bears my name.'

'I see that I hold a sanctuary in their hearts, I see her, an old woman, weeping for me on the anniversary of this day.

'I see a man bringing a boy to this place – fair to look upon, with not a trace of this day's disfigurement – and I hear him tell the child my story, with a tender and a faltering voice.

'It is a far, far better thing that I do, than I have ever done; it is a far, far better rest that I go to than I have ever known.'

A Tale of Two Cities

8
The Black Veil

This is a short story by Dickens, written under the pen-name 'Boz' when he was in his early twenties.

One winter's evening, towards the close of the year 1800, a young medical practitioner, recently established in business, was seated by a cheerful fire in his little parlour, listening to the wind which was beating the rain against the window, or rumbling in the chimney. The night was wet and cold; he had been walking through mud and water the whole day, and was now in his dressing-gown and slippers, more than half asleep and less than half awake, revolving a thousand matters in his wandering imagination. First, he thought how hard the wind was blowing, and how the cold, sharp rain would be at that moment beating in his face, if he were not comfortably housed at home. Then, he thought how happy it would make Rose if he could only tell her that he had found a patient at last, and hoped to have more, and to come down again, and marry her, and take her home to gladden his lonely fireside. Then, he began to wonder when his first patient would appear, or whether he was destined never to have any patients at all; and then, he thought about Rose again, and dropped to sleep and dreamed about her, till the tones of her sweet merry voice sounded in his ears, and her soft tiny hand rested on his shoulder.

There *was* a hand upon his shoulder, but it was neither soft nor tiny; its owner being a corpulent round-headed boy, who, in consideration of the sum of one shilling per week and his food, was let out by the parish.

'A lady, sir – a lady!' whispered the boy, rousing his master with a shake.

'What lady?' cried our friend, starting up, not quite certain that his dream was an illusion, and half expecting that it might be Rose herself – 'What lady? Where?'

'*There*, sir!' replied the boy, pointing to the glass door leading into the surgery.

The surgeon looked towards the door, and started himself, for an instant, on beholding the appearance of his visitor.

It was a singularly tall woman, dressed in deep mourning, and standing so close to the door that her face almost touched the glass. The upper part of her figure was muffled in a black shawl, as if for the purpose of concealment; and her face was shrouded by a thick black veil. She stood perfectly erect, her figure was drawn up to its full height, and though the surgeon *felt* that the eyes beneath the veil were fixed on him, she stood perfectly motionless.

'Do you wish to consult me?' he inquired, with some hesitation, holding open the door. It opened inwards, and therefore the action did not alter the position of the figure, which still remained motionless on the same spot.

She slightly inclined her head.

'Pray walk in,' said the surgeon.

The figure moved a step forward; and then, turning its head, appeared to hesitate.

'Leave the room, Tom,' said the young man. 'Draw the curtain, and shut the door.'

The boy drew a green curtain across the glass part of the door, retired into the surgery, closed the door after him, and immediately applied one of his large eyes to the keyhole on the other side.

The surgeon drew a chair to the fire, and motioned the visitor to a seat. The mysterious figure slowly moved towards it. As the blaze shone upon the black dress, the surgeon observed that the bottom of it was saturated with mud and rain.

'You are very wet,' he said.

'I am,' said the stranger, in a low deep voice.

'And you are ill?' added the surgeon, compassionately, for the tone was that of a person in pain.

'I am,' was the reply – 'very ill; not bodily, but mentally. It is not for myself, or on my own behalf,' continued the stranger, 'that I come to you. If I laboured under bodily disease, I should not be out, alone, at such an hour, or on such a night as this. It is for another that I beseech your aid, sir. I may be mad to ask it for him – I think I am; but, night after night, through the long dreary hours of watching and weeping, the thought has been ever present to my mind; and though even *I* see the hopelessness of human assistance **availing** him, the bare thought of laying him in his grave without it makes my blood run cold!' And a shudder trembled through the speaker's frame.

There was a desperate earnestness in this woman's manner, that went to the young man's heart. He was young in his profession, and had not yet witnessed enough of the miseries which are daily presented be-

Glossary

availing: helping

fore the eyes of its members, to have grown comparatively callous to human suffering.

'If,' he said, rising hastily, 'the person of whom you speak, be in so hopeless a condition as you describe, not a moment is to be lost. I will go with you instantly. Why did you not obtain medical advice before?'

'Because it would have been useless before – because it is useless even now,' replied the woman, clasping her hands passionately.

The surgeon gazed, for a moment, on the black veil, as if to ascertain the expression of the features beneath it; its thickness, however, rendered such a result impossible.

'You *are* ill,' he said, gently, 'although you do not know it. The fever, the fatigue you have evidently undergone, is burning within you now. Put that to your lips,' he continued, pouring out a glass of water – 'compose yourself for a few moments, and then tell me, as calmly as you can, what the disease of the patient is, and how long he has been ill. When I know what is necessary to render my visit serviceable to him, I am ready to accompany you.'

The stranger lifted the glass of water to her mouth, without raising the veil; put it down again untasted; and burst into tears.

'I know,' she said, sobbing aloud, 'that what I say to you now, seems like the ravings of fever. I have been told so before, less kindly than by you. I am not a young woman; My natural term of life cannot be many years longer, and should be dear on that account; but I would lay it down without a sigh – with cheerfulness – with joy – if what I tell you now were only false or imaginary. Tomorrow morning he of whom I speak will be, I *know*, though I would **fain** think otherwise, beyond the reach of human aid; and yet, tonight, though he is in deadly peril, you must not see, and could not serve, him.'

'I am unwilling to increase your distress,' said the surgeon, after a short pause, 'by making any comment on what you have just said, or to investigate a subject you are so anxious to conceal; but there is an inconsistency in your statement. This person is dying tonight, and I cannot see him when my assistance might possibly avail; you **apprehend** it will be useless tomorrow, and yet you would have me see him then! If he be, indeed, as dear to you as your words and manner would imply, why not try to save his life before delay and his disease render it impracticable?'

'God help me!' exclaimed the woman, weeping bitterly, 'how can I hope strangers will believe what appears incredible, even to myself? You will *not* see him then, sir?' she added, rising suddenly.

'I did not say that I declined to see him,' replied the surgeon; 'but I warn you, that if you persist in this **procrastination**, and the individual dies, a fearful responsibility rests with you.'

'The responsibility will rest heavily somewhere,' replied the stranger bitterly. 'Whatever responsibility rests with me, I am content to bear, and ready to answer.'

'I will see him in the morning, if you leave me the address. At what hour can he be seen?'

'*Nine*,' replied the stranger.

Glossary

fain: willingly, gladly
apprehend: believe, know
procrastination: deliberate delay, time-wasting

'You must excuse me pressing these inquiries,' said the surgeon. 'But is he in your charge now?'

'He is not,' was the rejoinder.

'Then, if I gave you instructions for his treatment through the night, you could not assist him?'

The woman wept bitterly, as she replied, 'I could not.'

Finding that there was little prospect of obtaining more information; and anxious to spare the woman's feelings, which were most painful to witness; the surgeon repeated his promise of calling in the morning at the appointed hour. His visitor, after giving him a direction to an **obscure** part of Walworth, left the house in the same mysterious manner in which she had entered it.

It will be readily believed that so extraordinary a visit produced a considerable impression on the mind of the young surgeon; and that he speculated a great deal and to very little purpose on the possible circumstances of the case. He had often heard instances, in which a **presentiment** of death, at a particular day, or even minute, had been entertained and realized. At one moment he was inclined to think that the present might be such a case; but then it occurred to him that all the **anecdotes** of the kind he had ever heard, were of persons who had been troubled with a foreboding of their own death. This woman, however, spoke of another person – a man; and it was impossible to suppose that a mere dream or delusion of fancy would induce her to speak with such terrible certainty as she had spoken. It could not be that the man was to be murdered in the morning, and that the woman, originally a consenting party, and bound to secrecy by an oath, had relented, and had determined to prevent his death if possible, by the timely interposition of medical aid? The idea of such things happening within two miles of the metropolis appeared preposterous. Then, his original impression that the woman's intellects were disordered, recurred; and, he made up his mind to believe that she was mad. Certain misgivings upon this point, however, stole upon his thoughts at the time, and presented themselves again and again through the long dull course of a sleepless night; during which, in spite of all his efforts to the contrary, he was unable to banish the black veil from his disturbed imagination.

The back part of Walworth is a straggling miserable place, even in these days; but, five-and-thirty years ago, it was little better than a dreary waste, inhabited by a few scattered people of questionable character, whose poverty prevented their living in any better neighbourhood, or whose mode of life rendered its solitude desirable.

The appearance of the place through which he walked in the morning, was not calculated to raise the spirits of the young surgeon, or to dispel any feeling of anxiety or depression which the singular kind of visit he was about to make, had awakened. Striking off from the high road, his way lay across a marshy common, through irregular lanes, with here and there a ruinous and dismantled cottage fast falling to pieces with decay and neglect. A stunted tree, or pool of stagnant water skirted the path occasionally; and, now

Glossary

obscure: concealed, little-known
presentiment: foreknowledge, glimpse into the future
anecdotes: stories, usually of a personal nature

and then, a miserable patch of garden-ground, with a few old boards knocked together for a summer-house, and old palings imperfectly mended with stakes pilfered from the neighbouring hedges, bore testimony to the poverty of the inhabitants, and the little scruple they entertained in appropriating the property of other people to their own use. Occasionally, a filthy-looking woman would make her appearance from the door of a dirty house, to empty the contents of some cooking utensil into the gutter in front, or to scream after a little slip-shod girl, who had contrived to stagger a few yards from the door under the weight of a sallow infant almost as big as herself; but scarcely anything was stirring around; the cold damp mist which hung heavily over it, presented a lonely and dreary appearance perfectly in keeping with the objects we have described.

After plodding wearily through the mud and mire; making many inquiries for the place to which he had been directed; the young man at length arrived before the house which had been pointed out to him. It was a small low building, one story above the ground, with a desolate and unpromising exterior. An old yellow curtain was closely drawn across the window upstairs, and the parlour shutters were closed, but not fastened. The house was detached from any other, and there was no other habitation in sight.

The surgeon hesitated, and walked a few paces beyond the house, before he could **prevail upon** himself to lift the knocker. Even the streets in the gayest parts of London were imperfectly lighted at that time; and such places as these were left entirely to the mercy of the moon and stars. The chances of detecting desperate characters, or of tracing them to their haunts, were thus rendered very few, and their offences naturally increased in boldness. Be this as it may, whatever reflection made him hesitate, he *did* hesitate: but, being a young man of strong mind and personal courage, it was only for an instant; – he stepped briskly back and knocked gently at the door.

A low whispering was audible, immediately afterwards, as if some person at the end of the passage were conversing stealthily with another on the landing above. It was succeeded by the noise of a pair of heavy boots upon the bare floor. The door-chain was unfastened; the door opened; and a tall man, with black hair, and a face as pale and haggard as any dead man, presented himself.

'Walk in, sir,' he said in a low tone.

The surgeon did so, and the man having secured the door again, by the chain, led the way to a small back parlour at the extremity of the passage.

'Am I in time?'

'Too soon!' replied the man. The surgeon turned hastily round, with a gesture of astonishment mixed with alarm.

'If you'll step in here, sir,' said the man, 'if you'll step in here, sir, you won't be detained five minutes, I assure you.'

The surgeon at once walked into the room. The man closed the door, and left him alone.

It was a little cold room, with no other furniture than two chairs, and a table. A handful of fire, unguarded by any fender, was burning in the grate, which brought out the damp if it served no more comfortable purpose, for the unwholesome moisture was

---

Glossary

prevail upon: force

stealing down the walls, in long slug-like tracks. The window, which was broken and patched in many places, looked into a small enclosed piece of ground, almost covered with water. Not a sound was to be heard, either within the house or without. The young surgeon sat down by the fireplace, to await the result of his first professional visit.

He had not remained in this position many minutes, when the noise of some approaching vehicle struck his ear. It stopped; the street door was opened; a low talking succeeded, accompanied with a shuffling noise of footsteps, along the passage and on the stairs, as if two or three men were engaged in carrying some heavy body to the room above. The creaking of the stairs, a few seconds afterwards, announced that the newcomers having completed their task, were leaving the house. The door was again closed, and the former silence was restored.

Another five minutes elapsed, and the surgeon resolved to explore the house, in search of some one to whom he might make his errand known, when the room door opened, and his last night's visitor, dressed in exactly the same manner, with the veil lowered as before, motioned him to advance. The singular height of her form, coupled with the circumstance of her not speaking, caused the idea to pass across his brain for an instant, that it might be a man disguised in woman's attire. The sobs which issued from beneath the veil, and the attitude of grief of the whole figure, however, at once exposed the absurdity of the suspicion; and he hastily followed.

The woman led the way upstairs to the front room, and paused at the door, to let him enter first. It was scantily furnished with a few chairs, and a bedstead, covered with a patchwork counterpane. The dim light admitted through the curtain which he had noticed from the outside, rendered the objects in the room so indistinct, that he did not, at first, perceive the object on which his eye at once rested when the woman rushed frantically past him, and flung herself on her knees by the bedside.

Stretched upon the bed, in a linen wrapper, and covered with blankets, lay a human form, stiff and motionless. The head and face, which were those of a man, were uncovered, save by a bandage which passed over the head and under the chin. The eyes were closed. The left arm lay heavily across the bed, and the woman held the passive hand.

The surgeon gently pushed the woman aside, and took the hand in his.

'My God!' he exclaimed, letting it fall – 'the man is dead!'

The woman started to her feet and beat her hands together. 'Oh! don't say so, sir,' she exclaimed, with a burst of passion, amounting almost to frenzy. 'Oh! don't say so, sir! I can't bear it! Men have been brought to life, before, when unskilful people have given them up for lost; and men have died, who might have been restored, if proper means had been resorted to. Don't let him lie here, sir, without one effort to save him! This very moment life may be passing away. Do try, sir, – do, for Heaven's sake!' – And while speaking, she hurriedly chafed, first the forehead, and then the breast, of the senseless form before her; and then, wildly beat the cold hands, which, when she ceased to hold them, fell listlessly and heavily back on the coverlet.

'It is of no use,' said the surgeon, soothingly, as he withdrew his hand from the man's breast. 'Stay – undraw that curtain!'

'Why?' said the woman, starting up.

'Undraw that curtain!' repeated the surgeon in an agitated tone.

'*I* darkened the room on purpose,' said the woman, throwing herself before him as he rose to undraw it. – 'Oh! sir, have pity on me! If it can be of no use, and he is really dead, do not expose that form to other eyes than mine!'

'This man died no natural or easy death,' said the surgeon. 'I *must* see the body!' With a motion so sudden, that the woman hardly knew that he had slipped from beside her, he tore open the curtain, admitted the full light of day, and returned to the bedside.

'There has been violence here,' he said, pointing towards the body, and gazing intently on the face, from which the black veil was now, for the first time, removed. In the excitement of a minute before, the female had thrown off the bonnet and veil, and now stood with her eyes fixed upon him. Her features were those of a woman about fifty, who had once been handsome. Sorrow and weeping had left traces upon them which not time itself would ever have produced without their aid; her face was deadly pale; and there was a nervous contortion of the lip, and an unnatural fire in her eye, which showed too plainly that her bodily and mental powers had nearly sunk beneath an accumulation of misery.

'There has been violence here,' said the surgeon, preserving his searching glance.

'There has!' replied the woman.

'This man has been murdered.'

'That I call God to witness he has,' said the woman, passionately; 'pitilessly, inhumanly murdered!'

'By whom?' said the surgeon, seizing the woman by the arm.

'Look at the butchers' marks, and then ask me!' she replied.

The surgeon turned his face towards the bed, and bent over the body which now lay full in the light of the window. The throat was swollen, and a livid mark encircled it. The truth flashed suddenly upon him.

'This is one of the men who were hanged this morning!' he exclaimed, turning away with a shudder.

'It is,' replied the woman, with a cold, unmeaning stare.

'Who was he?' inquired the surgeon.

'*My son*,' rejoined the woman; and fell senseless at his feet.

The Black Veil

9
Dickens the observer and commentator: non-fiction

Dickens began his writing career as a journalist in London, finding an interest in people and places many would find unattractive. He explored parts of London his readers would not live in or visit themselves – back-streets of lower-class poverty, violence and dirt. For well-off readers in comfortable homes, Dickens was a literary guide to the lives which could be glimpsed – and passed by – on the streets of the capital. Sometimes he used details of low life to jolt the well-off reader, to show how other people lived. Dickens was both an objective reporter, and a sympathetic defender of people he wrote about. The descriptions of Newgate prison, for example, informs the reader and conveys a forceful message about social conditions and their effects on people.

As an observer, Dickens used social occasions and popular pleasures of the day to describe people as a species as well as individuals. In *Bank Holiday at Greenwich Fair* he shows human beings at work and play, all out to make the most of the occasion, whether it's to make money or catch a partner. He enjoyed watching the tricks and strategies of con-men and of young men and women out to attract.

These examples of his early writing show Dickens as both a comic and serious observer of England at work and play. They show his passionate interest in detail. In the fiction writing of his later life, snatches of people at work and play provide a realistic background to the stories. For some readers, this background scenery is what makes him a great writer, because his novels create a picture of England, as well as being a gripping read …

Bank Holiday at Greenwich Fair

This account brings to life the sounds and sights and smells of the fairground in a vivid glimpse of how people enjoyed themselves long ago. Some things may seem quite familiar – such as the skilful patter of fairground sellers and their confidence tricks, and the willingness of holiday-makers to have a go, even if they always lose. His comic account of the melodrama, the macabre, sensational side-shows, people enjoying a night out, with a giddy mixture of romance, dancing and drink, may make readers think that things haven't changed much since Dickens' day.

The road to Greenwich during the whole of Easter Monday, is in a state of perpetual bustle and noise. Cabs, hackney-coaches, carts, coal-waggons, stages, omnibuses, sociables, gigs, donkey-chaises – all crammed with people roll along at their utmost speed; the dust flies in clouds, ginger-beer corks go off in volleys, the balcony of every public-house is crowded with people, smoking and drinking, half the private houses are turned into tea shops, fiddles are in great request, every little fruit shop displays its stall of **gilt** gingerbread and penny toys; horses won't go on, and wheels will come off; ladies in '**caravans**' scream with fright at every fresh concussion, and their admirers find it necessary to sit remarkably close to them, by way of encouragement; servants-of-all-work, who have got a holiday for the day, make the most of their time with the faithful admirer who waits for a stolen interview at the corner of the street every night, when they go to fetch the beer. Everybody is anxious to be at the fair, or in the park, as soon as possible.

The chief place of resort in the daytime, after the public-houses, is the park, in which the principal amusement is to drag young ladies up the steep hill which leads to the Observatory, and then drag them down again, at the very top of their speed, greatly to the **derangement** of their curls and bonnet-caps, and much to the **edification** of lookers-on from below. Love-sick **swains**, under the influence of gin-and-water, become violently affectionate: and the fair objects of their regard enhance the value of stolen kisses, by a vast deal of struggling, and holding down of heads, and cries of 'Oh! Ha' done, then, George – Oh, do tickle him for me, Mary – Well, I never!' Little old men and women, with a small basket under one arm, and a wine-glass in the other hand, tender 'A drop o' the right sort' to the different groups; and young ladies, who are persuaded to indulge in a drop display a pleasing degree of reluctance to taste it, and cough afterwards with great propriety.

But it grows dark: the crowd has gradually dispersed, and only a few stragglers are left behind. The light in the direction of the church shows that the fair is illuminated: and the distant noise proves it to be filling fast.

Glossary

gilt: gingerbread used to be decorated with thin gold leaf

'caravans': group travelling together

derangement: messing up, untidying

edification: (here) entertainment

swains: male admirers, boyfriends

Five minutes' walking brings you to the fair. The entrance is occupied on either side by the vendors of gingerbread and toys: the stalls are gaily lighted up, the most attractive goods **profusely** disposed, and unbonneted young ladies seize you by the coat, and use all the **blandishments** of 'Do, dear' – 'There's a love' – 'Don't be cross, now,' etc., to induce you to purchase half a pound of the real spice nuts, of which the majority of the regular fair-goers carry a pound or two as a present supply, tied up in a cotton pocket- handkerchief. Occasionally you pass a deal table, on 'which are exposed pen'orths of pickled salmon in little white saucers: oysters, with shells as large as cheese-plates, and **divers** specimens of a species of snail (*wilks*, we think they are called), floating in a **bilious**-looking green liquid. Cigars, too, are in great demand; gentlemen must smoke, of course, and here they are, two a penny, in a regular authentic cigar-box, with a lighted tallow candle in the centre.

Imagine yourself in an extremely dense crowd, which swings you to and fro, and in and out, and every way but the right one; add to this the screams of women, the shouts of boys, the clanging of gongs, the firing of pistols, the ringing of bells, the noise of a dozen bands, with three drums in each, all playing different tunes at the same time, the hallooing of showmen, and an occasional roar from the wild-beast shows; and you are in the very centre and heart of the fair.

This immense booth, with the large stage in front, so brightly illuminated with lamps, is 'Richardson's,' where you have a melodrama (with three murders and a ghost), a pantomime, a comic song, an overture, and some incidental music, all done in five-and-twenty minutes.

The company are now promenading outside in all the dignity of wigs, spangles, **red-ochre**, and

whitening. See with what a ferocious air the gentleman who personates the Mexican chief, paces up and
down, and with what an eye of calm dignity the principal **tragedian** gazes on the crowd below, or con-
verses confidentially with the **harlequin**! The four
clowns, who are engaged in a mock broadsword com-
bat, may be all very well for the low-minded holiday-
makers; but these are the people for the reflective
portion of the community. They look so noble in those
Roman dresses, with their yellow legs and arms, long
black curly heads, bushy eyebrows, and scowl expres-
sive of assassination, and vengeance, and everything
else that is grand and solemn. Then, the ladies – were
there ever such innocent and awful-looking beings; as
they walk up and down the platform in twos and
threes, with their arms round each other's waists, or
leaning for support on one of those majestic men!
Their spangled muslin dresses and blue satin shoes
and sandals are the admiration of all beholders; and
the playful manner in which they check the advances
of the clown, is perfectly enchanting.

'Just a-going to begin! Pray come for'erd, come
for'erd,' exclaims the man in the countryman's dress,
for the seventieth time: and people force their way up

Glossary

profusely: plentifully
blandishments: flattering or coaxing words
divers: various
bilious: sickly, makes you feel queasy
red-ochre, whitening: stage make-up
tragedian: actor playing a tragic part
harlequin: brightly dressed stage character

the steps in crowds. The band suddenly strikes up. 'All in to begin,' shouts the manager, when no more people can be induced to 'come for'erd,' and away rush the leading members of the company to do the dreadful in the first piece.

A change of performances takes place every day during the fair, but the story of the tragedy is always pretty much the same. There is a rightful heir, who loves a young lady, and is beloved by her; and the wrongful heir gets hold of the rightful heir, and throws him into a dungeon, just to kill him off when convenient, for which purpose he hires a couple of assassins – a good one and a bad one – who, the moment they are left alone, get up a little murder on their own account, the good one killing the bad one, and the bad one wounding the good one. Then the rightful heir is discovered in prison, carefully holding a long chain in his hands, and seated **despondingly** in a large arm-chair; and the young lady comes in to two bars of soft music, and embraces the rightful heir; and then the wrongful heir comes in to two bars of quick music and goes on in the most shocking manner, throwing the young lady about as if she was nobody, and calling the rightful heir 'Ar-recreant – ar-wretch!' in a very loud voice, which answers the double purpose of displaying his passion, and preventing the sound being deadened by the sawdust. The interest becomes intense; the wrongful heir draws his sword, and rushes on the rightful heir; a blue smoke is seen, a gong is heard, and a tall white figure (who has been all this time, behind the arm-chair, covered over with a table-cloth), slowly rises to the tune of 'Oft in the stilly night.' This is no other than the ghost of the rightful heir's father, who was killed by the wrongful heir's father, at sight of which the wrongful heir becomes **apoplectic**, and is literally 'struck all of a heap,' the stage not being large enough to admit of his falling down at full length. Then the good assassin staggers in, and says he was hired in conjunction with the bad assassin, by the wrongful heir, to kill the rightful heir; and he's killed a good many people in his time, but he's very sorry for it, and won't do so any more – a promise which he immediately redeems, by dying off hand without any nonsense about it. Then the rightful heir throws down his chain; and then two men, a sailor, and a young woman come in, and the ghost makes dumb motions to them, which they, by supernatural interference, understand – for no one else can; and the ghost (who can't do anything without blue fire) blesses the rightful heir and the young lady, by half suffocating them with smoke: and then a bell rings, and the curtain drops.

The exhibitions next in popularity to these **itinerant** theatres are the travelling 'Wild-beast shows,' where a military band in beef-eater's costume, with leopard-skin caps, play incessantly; and where large highly-coloured representations of tigers tearing men's heads open, and a lion being burnt with red-hot irons to induce him to drop his victim, are hung up outside, by way of attracting visitors.

The principal officer at these places is generally a very tall, hoarse man, in a scarlet coat, with a cane in his hand, with which he occasionally raps the pictures

---

Glossary

despondingly: losing hope
apoplectic: being speechless in a fit of rage
itinerant: travelling

we have just noticed, by way of illustrating his description – something in this way. 'Here, here, here; the lion, the lion (tap), exactly as he is represented on the canvas outside (three taps): no waiting, remember; no deception. The fe-ro-cious lion (tap, tap) who bit off the gentleman's head and has killed on the average three keepers a year ever since he arrived at matoority. No extra charge on this account; the price of admission is only sixpence. This address never fails to produce a considerable sensation, and sixpences flow into the treasury with wonderful rapidity.

The dwarfs are also objects of great curiosity, and as a dwarf, a giantess, a living skeleton, a wild Indian, 'a young lady of singular beauty, with perfectly white hair and pink eyes,' and two or three other natural curiosities, are usually exhibited together for the small charge of a penny, they attract very numerous audiences. The best thing about a dwarf is, that he has always a little box, about two feet six inches high, into which, by long practice, he can just manage to get, by doubling himself up; this box is painted outside like a six-roomed house, and as the crowd see him ring a bell, or fire a pistol out of the first-floor window, they **verily** believe that it is his ordinary town residence, divided like other mansions into drawing-rooms, dining-parlour, and bedchambers. Shut up in this case, the unfortunate little object is brought out to delight the throng by holding a **facetious** dialogue with the **proprietor**: in the course of which, the dwarf (who is always particularly drunk) pledges himself to sing a comic song inside, and pays various compliments to the ladies, which induce them to 'come for'erd' with great alacrity. As a giant is not so easily moved, a pair of **indescribables** of most **capacious** dimensions, and a huge shoe, are usually brought out, into which two or three stout men get all at once, to the enthusiastic delight of the crowd, who are quite satisfied with the solemn assurance that these **habiliment**s form part of the giant's everyday costume.

The grandest and most numerously-frequented booth in the whole fair, however, is 'The Crown and Anchor' – a temporary ball-room – we forget how many hundred feet long, the price of admission to which is one shilling. Immediately on your right hand as you enter, after paying your money, is a refreshment place, at which cold beef, roast and boiled, French rolls, stout, wine, tongue, ham, even fowls are displayed in tempting array. There is a raised orchestra, and the place is boarded all the way down, in patches, just wide enough for a country dance.

There is no master of the ceremonies in this artificial Eden – all is primitive, unreserved, and unstudied. The dust is blinding, the heat **insupportable**, the company somewhat noisy, and in the highest spirits possible: the ladies, in the height of their innocent animation, dancing in the gentlemen's hats, and the gentlemen promenading in the ladies' bonnets, or with the more expensive ornaments of false noses,

Glossary

verily: truly

facetious: meant to be funny but in fact rather silly

proprietor: owner

indescribables: (here) underwear

capacious: roomy

habiliments: clothes

insupportable: unbearable

The place is boarded all the way down ... just wide enough for a country dance.

and low-crowned hats: playing children's drums, and accompanied by ladies on the penny trumpet.

The noise of these various instruments, the orchestra, the shouting and the dancing, is perfectly bewildering. The dancing itself beggars description – every figure lasts about an hour, and the ladies bounce up and down the middle, with a degree of spirit which is quite indescribable. As to the gentlemen, they stamp their feet against the ground, go down the middle and up again, with cigars in their mouths, and silk handkerchiefs in their hands, and whirl their partners round, scrambling and falling, and embracing, and knocking up against the other couples, until they are fairly tired out, and can move no longer. The same scene is repeated again and again until a late hour at night: and a great many clerks and 'prentices find themselves next morning with aching heads, empty pockets, damaged hats, and a very imperfect recollection of how it was they did *not* get home.

Sketches by Boz

A visit to Newgate prison

There are prison scenes in many of Dickens' novels. Here he takes readers on a guided tour, pointing out the reality of the death penalty. His gruesome description of the last hours and thoughts and feelings of the condemned are designed to make the reader feel sympathy. It's not that he wants readers to sympathize with criminals, but he wants to show that capital punishment is barbaric as well as useless in stopping crime. As a journalist here, and as a novelist elsewhere, he tries to stop readers from trusting easy answers to social problems.

Scarcely one man out of a hundred, whose road to business every morning lies through Newgate Street, or the Old Bailey, would pass the building without a hasty glance on its small, grated windows, and a thought upon the condition of the unhappy beings in its dismal cells; and yet these same men, day by day, and hour by hour, pass and repass this gloomy **depository** of the guilt and misery of London, in one perpetual stream of life and bustle, utterly unmindful of the throng of wretched creatures pent up within it – nay, not even knowing, or if they do, not heeding, the fact, that as they pass one particular angle of the massive wall with a light laugh or a merry whistle, they stand within one yard of a fellow creature, bound and helpless, whose hours are numbered, from whom the last feeble ray of hope has fled for ever, and whose miserable career will shortly terminate in a violent and shameful death. Contact with death, even in its least terrible shape, is solemn and appalling. How much more awful is it to reflect on this near **vicinity** to the dying – to men in full health and vigour, in the flower of youth or the prime of life, with all their faculties as acute and perfect as your own; but dying, nevertheless – dying as surely – with the hand of death imprinted upon them as **indelibly** – as if mortal disease had wasted their frames to shadows, and **corruption** had already begun!

It was with some such thoughts as these that we determined, not many weeks since, to visit the interior of Newgate and proceed to lay its results before our readers, in the hope that this paper may not be found wholly devoid of interest. We have only to **premise**, that we do not intend to fatigue the reader with any statistical accounts of the prison; they will be found at length in reports of committees and authorities of equal weight. We took no notes, made no memoranda, measured none of the yards, ascertained the exact number of inches in no particular room: are unable even to report of how many apartments the gaol is composed.

We saw the prison, and saw the prisoners; and what we did see, and what we thought, we will tell at once in our own way.

Glossary

depository: place where something is left
vicinity: closeness, proximity
indelibly: cannot be removed, permanently fixed
corruption: rotting of the body, decomposition
premise: state

The prison chapel is situated at the back of the governor's house: the latter having no windows looking into the interior of the prison. Whether the associations connected with the place – the knowledge that here a portion of the burial service is, on some dreadful occasions, performed over the **quick** and not upon the dead – cast over it a still more gloomy and sombre air than art has imparted to it, we know not, but its appearance is very striking. The **meanness of its appointments** – the bare and scanty pulpit, with the paltry painted pillars on either side – the women's gallery with its great heavy curtain – the men's with its unpainted benches and dingy front – the tottering little table at the altar, with the commandments on the wall above it, scarcely legible through lack of paint, and dust and damp – are strange and striking. There is one object, too, which rivets the attention and fascinates the gaze, and from which we may turn horror-stricken in vain, for the recollection of it will haunt us, waking and sleeping, for a long time afterwards. Immediately below the reading-desk, on the floor of the chapel, and forming the most conspicuous object in its little area, is *the condemned pew*; a huge black pen, in which the wretched people, who are singled out for death, are placed on the Sunday preceding their execution, in sight of all their fellow prisoners, from many of whom they may have been separated but a week before, to hear prayers for their own souls, to join in the responses of their own burial service, and to listen to an address, warning their recent companions to take example by their fate, and urging themselves, while there is yet time – nearly four-and-twenty hours – to 'turn, and flee from the wrath to come!' Imagine the feelings of the men whom that fearful pew has enclosed, and of whom no mortal remnant may now remain! Think of the hopeless clinging to life to the last, and the wild despair, far exceeding in anguish the felon's death itself, by which they have heard the certainty of their speedy transmission to another world, with all their crimes upon their heads, rung into their ears by the officiating clergyman!

At one time – and at no distant period either – the coffins of the men about to be executed, were placed in that pew, upon the seat by their side, during the whole service. It may seem incredible, but it is true. Let us hope that the increased spirit of civilization and humanity which abolished this frightful and degrading custom, may extend itself to other **usages** equally barbarous; usages which have not even the **plea of utility** in their defence, as every year's experience has shown them to be more and more **inefficacious.**

Leaving the chapel, and crossing the yard, the visitor arrives at a thick iron gate of great size and strength. Having been admitted through it by the **turnkey** on duty, he turns sharp round to the left, and pauses before another gate; and, having passed this

┌ Glossary

quick: people who are alive

meanness of its appointments: bare decorations and furnishings

usages: customs, beliefs

plea of utility: the excuse of being useful

inefficacious: ineffective

turnkey: gaoler, someone who locks and unlocks the prison door

last barrier, he stands in the most terrible part of this gloomy building – the condemned ward.

At the upper end is a cistern of water, and at the bottom a double grating similar to that before described. Through these grates the prisoners are allowed to see their friends; a turnkey always remaining in the vacant space between, during the whole interview. Immediately on the right as you enter, is a building containing the day-room and cells; the yard is on every side surrounded by lofty walls; and the whole is under the constant inspection of vigilant and experienced turnkeys.

In the first apartment into which we were conducted were five-and-twenty or thirty prisoners, all under sentence of death – men of all ages and appearances, from a hardened old offender with swarthy face and grizzly beard of three days' growth, to a handsome boy, not fourteen years old, and of singularly youthful appearance even for that age, who had been condemned for burglary.

In the room below were three men, the nature of whose offence rendered it necessary to separate them even from their companions in guilt. It is a long, sombre room, with two windows sunk into the stone wall, and here the wretched men are pinioned on the morning of their execution, before moving towards the scaffold. The fate of one of these prisoners was uncertain; some **mitigatory** circumstances having come to light since his trial. The other two had nothing to expect from the mercy of the crown; their doom was sealed; no plea could be urged in **extenuation** of their crime, and they well knew that for them there was no hope in this world. 'The two short ones,' the turnkey whispered, 'were dead men.'

The man to whom we have alluded as entertaining some hopes of escape, was lounging, at the greatest distance he could place between himself and his companions, in the window nearest to the door. He was probably aware of our approach, and had assumed an air of courageous indifference; his face was purposely averted towards the window, and he stirred not an inch while we were present. The other two men were at the upper end of the room. One of them, who was imperfectly seen in the dim light, had his back towards us, and was stooping over the fire, with his right arm on the mantel-piece, and his head sunk upon it. The other was leaning on the sill of the farthest window. The light fell full upon his pale, haggard face, and disordered hair, an appearance which, at that distance, was ghastly. His cheek rested upon his hand; and, with his face a little raised, and his eyes wildly staring before him, he seemed to be unconsciously intent on counting the chinks in the opposite wall.

A few paces up the yard, lie the condemned cells. Prior to the recorder's report being made, all the prisoners under sentence of death are removed from the day-room at five o'clock in the afternoon, and locked up in these cells, where they are allowed a candle until ten o'clock; and here they remain until seven next morning. When the warrant for a prisoner's execution arrives, he is removed to the cells and confined in one of them until he leaves it for the scaffold. He is

---

Glossary

mitigatory: making less severe or serious
extenuation: making something appear less bad, excusing

Conceive the situation of a man, spending his last night on earth in this cell.

at liberty to walk in the yard; but, both in his walks and in his cell, he is constantly attended by a turnkey who never leaves him on any pretence.

We entered the first cell. It was a stone dungeon, eight feet long by six wide, with a bench at the upper end, under which were a common rug, a bible, and prayer book. An iron candlestick was fixed into the wall at the side; and a small high window in the back admitted as much air and light as could struggle in between a double row of heavy, crossed iron bars. It contained no other furniture of any description.

Conceive the situation of a man, spending his last night on earth in this cell. Buoyed up with some vague and undefined hope of reprieve, he knew not why – indulging in some wild idea of escaping, he knew not how – hour after hour of the three preceding days has fled with a speed which no man living would deem possible, for none but this dying man can know. He has wearied his friends with **entreaties**, exhausted the attendants with **importunities**, neglected in his feverish restlessness the timely warnings of his spiritual consoler; and, now that the illusion is at last dispelled, now that eternity is before him and guilt behind, now that his fears of death and an overwhelming sense of his helpless, hopeless state rushes upon him, he is lost and stupefied, and has neither thoughts to turn to, nor power to call upon, the Almighty Being, from whom alone he can seek mercy and forgiveness.

┌─ Glossary ─────────────────────

entreaties: desperate, begging requests
importunities: bothersome demands

Hours have glided by, and still he sits upon the same stone bench with folded arms, heedless alike of the fast decreasing time before him, and the urgent entreaties of the good man at his side. The feeble light is wasting gradually, and the deathlike stillness of the street without, broken only by the rumbling of some passing vehicle which echoes mournfully through the empty yards, warns him that the night is waning fast away. The deep bell of St Paul's strikes – one! He heard it; it has roused him. Seven hours left! He paces the narrow limits of his cell with rapid strides, cold drops of terror starting on his forehead, and every muscle of his frame quivering with agony. Seven hours! He suffers himself to be led to his seat, mechanically takes the bible which is placed in his hand, and tries to read and listen. No: his thoughts will wander. The book is torn and soiled by use – and like the book he read his lessons in, at school, just forty years ago! He has never bestowed a thought upon it, perhaps, since he left it as a child: and yet the place, the time, the room – nay, the very boys he played with, crowd as vividly before him as if they were scenes of yesterday; and some forgotten phrase, some childish word, rings in his ears like the echo of one uttered but a minute since. The voice of the clergyman recalls him to himself. He is reading from the sacred book its solemn promises of pardon for repentance, and its awful denuciation of **obdurate** men. He falls upon his knees and clasps his hands to pray. Hush! what sound was that? He starts upon his feet. It cannot be two yet. Hark! Two quarters have struck; – the third – the fourth. It is! Six hours left. Tell him not of repentance! Six hours' repentance for eight times six years of guilt and sin! He buries his face in his hands, and throws himself on the bench.

Worn with watching and excitement, he sleeps, and the same unsettled state of mind pursues him in his dreams. An **insupportable** load is taken from his breast; he is walking with his wife in a pleasant field, with the bright sky above them, and a fresh and boundless prospect on every side – how different from the stone walls of Newgate! She is looking – not as she did when he saw her for the last time in that dreadful place, but as she used when he loved her – long, long ago, before misery and ill-treatment had altered her looks, and vice had changed his nature, and she is leaning upon his arm, and looking up into his face with tenderness and affection – and he does *not* strike her now, nor rudely shake her from him. And oh! how glad he is to tell her all he had forgotten in that last hurried interview, and to fall on his knees before her and fervently beseech her pardon for all the unkindness and cruelty that wasted her form and broke her heart! The scene suddenly changes. He is on his trial again: there are the judge and jury, and prosecutors, and witnesses, just as they were before. How full the court is – what a sea of heads – with a gallows, too, and a scaffold, – and how all those people stare at *him*! Verdict, 'Guilty.' No matter: he will escape.

The night is dark and cold, the gates have been left open, and in an instant he is in the street, flying from his imprisonment like the wind. The streets are cleared, the open fields are gained and the broad wide country lies before him. Onward he dashes in the

Glossary

obdurate: stubbornly refusing to repent
insupportable: unbearable

midst of darkness, over hedge and ditch, through mud and pool, bounding with a speed and lightness, astonishing even to himself. At length he pauses; he must be safe from pursuit now; he will stretch himself on that bank and sleep till sunrise.

A period of unconsciousness succeeds. He wakes, cold and wretched. The dull grey light of morning is stealing into the cell, and falls upon the form of the attendant turnkey. Confused by his dreams, he starts from his uneasy bed in momentary uncertainty. It is but momentary. Every object in the narrow cell is too frightfully real to admit of doubt or mistake. He is the condemned felon again, guilty and despairing; and in two hours more will be dead.

Sketches by Boz